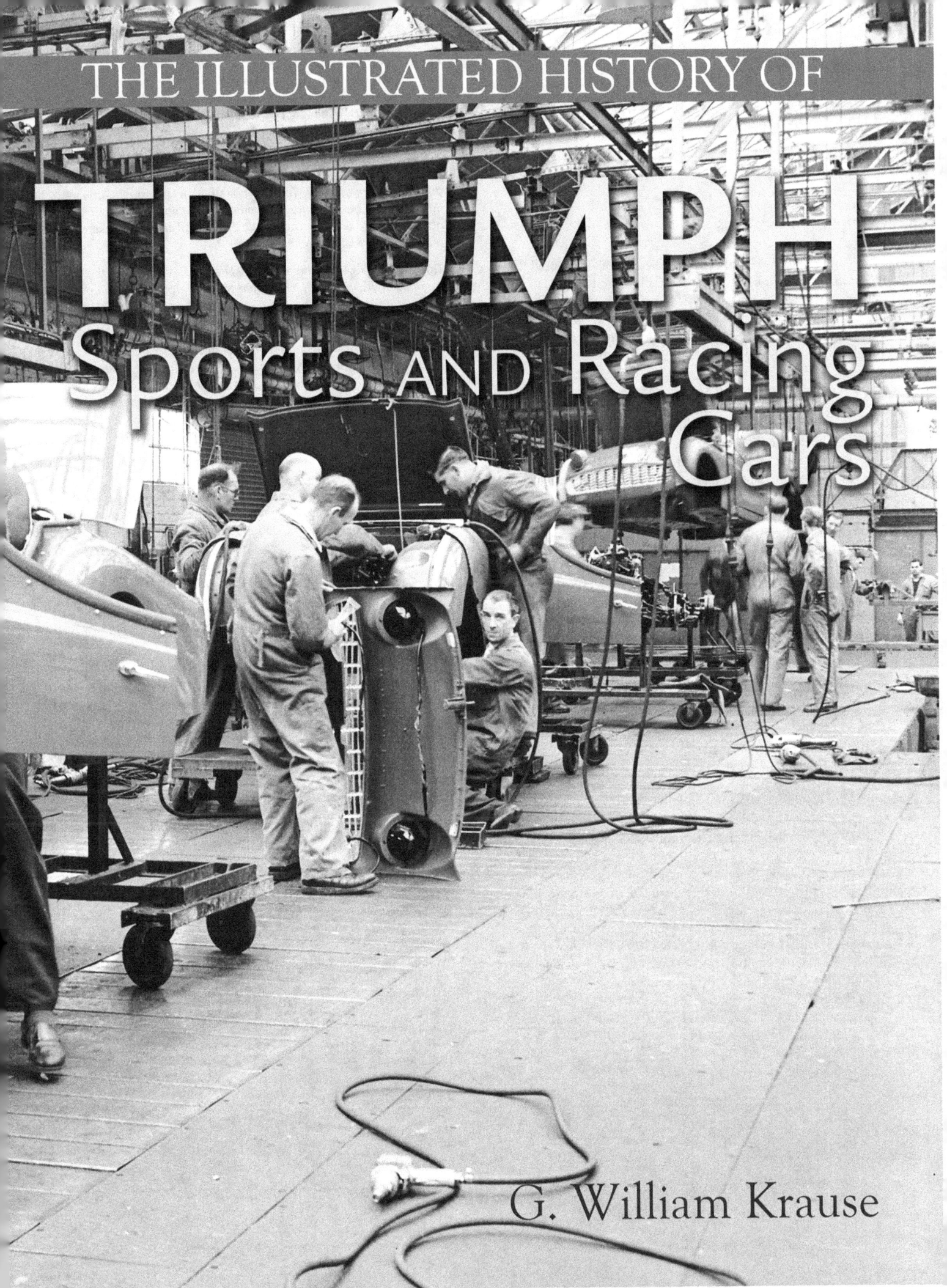

THE ILLUSTRATED HISTORY OF
TRIUMPH
Sports AND Racing Cars

G. William Krause

CarTech®

CarTech®, Inc.
6118 Main Street
North Branch, MN 55056
Phone: 651-277-1200 or 800-551-4754
Fax: 651-277-1203
www.cartechbooks.com

© 2017 by G. William Krause

All rights reserved. No part of this publication may be reproduced or utilized in any form or by any means, electronic or mechanical, including photocopying, recording, or by any information storage and retrieval system, without prior permission from the Publisher. All text, photographs, and artwork are the property of the Author unless otherwise noted or credited.

The information in this work is true and complete to the best of our knowledge. However, all information is presented without any guarantee on the part of the Author or Publisher, who also disclaim any liability incurred in connection with the use of the information and any implied warranties of merchantability or fitness for a particular purpose. Readers are responsible for taking suitable and appropriate safety measures when performing any of the operations or activities described in this work.

All trademarks, trade names, model names and numbers, and other product designations referred to herein are the property of their respective owners and are used solely for identification purposes. This work is a publication of CarTech, Inc., and has not been licensed, approved, sponsored, or endorsed by any other person or entity. The Publisher is not associated with any product, service, or vendor mentioned in this book, and does not endorse the products or services of any vendor mentioned in this book.

Edit by Bob Wilson
Layout by Monica Seiberlich

ISBN 9781613257814
Item No. CT596P

Library of Congress Cataloging-in-Publication Data
Names: Krause, G. William, author.
Title: The illustrated history of Triumph sports and racing cars / G. William
 Krause.
Description: Forest Lake, MN : CarTech, [2017] | Includes bibliographical
 references.
Identifiers: LCCN 2017003181 | ISBN 9781613253397
Subjects: LCSH: Triumph Motor Company. | Triumph automobile–History. |
 Sports cars–History.
Classification: LCC TL215.T7 K725 2017 | DDC 629.222--dc23
LC record available at https://lccn.loc.gov/2017003181

Written, edited, designed, and printed in the U.S.A.

Front Cover: *Introduced in 1961, the Triumph TR4 was the successor to the immensely popular sidescreen TR3s of the previous decade. The new models were designed by Italian Giovanni Michelotti and featured roll-up windows, better cockpit ventilation, and a much roomier trunk. The modern conveniences coupled with the contemporary styling made the new Triumph the most successful model to date.*

Frontispiece: *This 1956 TR3 illustrates the most significant design difference from the TR2. The egg-crate grille was brought forward to be flush with the front apron and trimmed to look more finished. A subsequent redesign of the apron for the TR3A explains why these cars are referred to as "small-mouth" 3s.*

Title Page: *TR3As on the assembly line in Coventry. This photo illustrates how the cars were bolted together from the inside out. The Girling disc brakes on the car in the foreground are being bled. (Photo Courtesy British Motor Industry Heritage Trust)*

Table of Contents: *The introduction of the final version of the GT6 was in 1970. Now known as Mark 3 around the world, the redesign brought the styling elements of the body in line with the rest of the Triumph line. The rear panel was used primarily on Spitfire Mark IV and Stag. The competition-style fuel cap was downsized and relocated to the left rear fender. This studio shot also features the new steel wheels with stamped fins. (Photo Courtesy British Motor Industry Heritage Trust)*

Back Cover Photos
Top: *Two common denominators are consistent throughout the history of Triumph's sports cars: short on time and short of capital. Yet somehow each successive car bested the previous model in style and appeal. The TR6 was no exception. The stunning design completely masked the fact that the center tub and many chassis components were carried forward from the TR250. (Photo Courtesy Classic Car Garage)*

Middle Left: *At long last an 8-cylinder version of the Wedge was announced for 1978. The TR8 featured the same handsome good looks, wind in the hair, and kick-in-the-pants performance that were hallmarks of the first TRs.*

Middle Right: *A removable hardtop was available on Spitfire from its inception. Two bolts on the windshield header and a few more at the back of the cockpit were all that needed to be tightened, and the car was airtight, although slightly claustrophobic. Here, a young couple illustrates the ease of installation. (Photo Courtesy British Motor Industry Heritage Trust)*

DISTRIBUTION BY:
Europe
PGUK
63 Hatton Garden
London EC1N 8LE, England
Phone: 020 7061 1980 • Fax: 020 7242 3725
www.pguk.co.uk

Australia
Renniks Publications Ltd.
3/37-39 Green Street
Banksmeadow, NSW 2109, Australia
Phone: 2 9695 7055 • Fax: 2 9695 7355
www.renniks.com

Canada
Login Canada
300 Saulteaux Crescent
Winnipeg, MB, R3J-3T2 Canada
Phone: 800 665 1148 • Fax: 800 665 0103
www.lb.ca

CONTENTS

Acknowledgments 6
Introduction 7

Chapter 1: Siegfried Bettmann and a Motorized Bicycle 9
Chapter 2: Triumph's First Sports Car 19
Chapter 3: The Italian Job 42
Chapter 4: What Began in Germany Returns to Germany 64
Chapter 5: Seventh Heaven: Triumph Gets a Wedgie 72
Chapter 6: The Bomb Goes Off 84
Chapter 7: Triumph on Track 106

Postscript: The Triumph Acclaim 124
Appendix: Production Totals 125
Resources and Recommended Reading 125
Index 126

DEDICATION

To my dad, George. Thank you for sharing your passion
and appreciation for these cars.

ACKNOWLEDGMENTS

Throughout this project I have met some really great people. Not just Triumph owners but car people in general. I have met many in person, others only via email. I hope to one day meet them all, face-to-face. Thank you all for your time and for sharing your cars and your knowledge.

I must thank a few folks for their help, knowledge, and guidance in seeing this book to fruition. First is Bob Wilson and the good people at CarTech for taking a chance on this subject, the British Motor Industry Heritage Trust, the VTR group, Triumphs of Minnesota, the British Car Club of Southwest Florida, Mark Brandow at Quality Coaches, REVs Institute, Simon Goldsworthy at *Triumph World* magazine, Marc Vorgers at Classic Car Garage, John Nikas at Moss Motors, Scott Marquis, Karl Stokes, John Allan, Mike Cook, Kas Kastner, Peter Brock, Tom Householder, Debbie Bradley, Bob Lee, Steve Shogren, John Allan, Doug Canfield, John Ridings Lee, David Gooley, my wife Katie and, of course, Dad and his stories.

INTRODUCTION

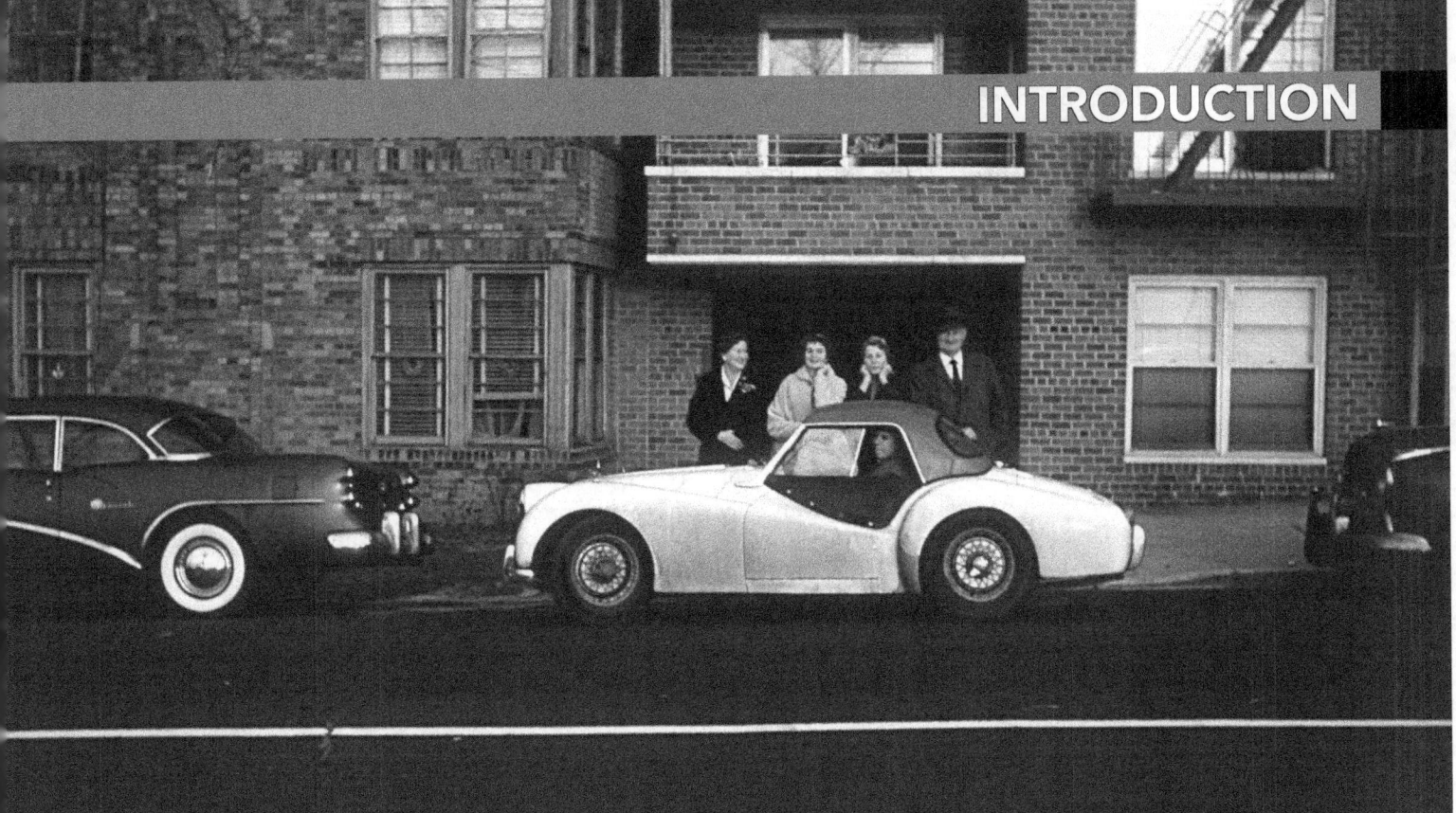

My father in his TR3 on Christmas Day 1958 in Brooklyn, New York. With the optional steel hardtop in place the car was a little more hospitable in winter, although the small heater still struggled to overcome the drafty side curtains. The car was a daily driver for more than seven years.

You might say that I was born into the British car family fold, and more specifically, Triumph cars. Although I have also owned MGs and Austin-Healeys through the years, my true allegiance belongs to the Coventry-based line of TRs, Spitfires, and GT6s.

This all began in the summer of 1960 with my first ride in a TR3. Unfortunately, it is not an unforgettable experience that is indelibly etched in my mind because I was on my mother's lap. The 1956 Triumph was their only car in those days, which was no small feat given the winters in Minnesota. No one recalls if the top was up or down; Dad was loath to put the top up. Just imagine how many of today's safety laws were violated that day.

A few years after that first fateful trip, the TR3 was put up on blocks and parked lengthwise at the back of the two-car garage. The two-seater could no longer support the growing family and the engine required a rebuild. The 2-liter was pulled with the best of intentions but sat neglected in the opposite corner of the garage.

As children, my brother and I sat in the car and pretended to be driving, I in the driver's seat, of course, with a jack handle poking through the hole in the transmission tunnel to serve as the make-believe shifter. Can you blame us? At the time, the car was so unique compared to anything on the road or in our garage. The cut doors, the cozy cockpit, the dashboard with a host of dials and gauges, and the small physical size.

Dad noticed my aptitude for cars and he began to share the lore of the sports car invasion in the 1950s. After all, he was right in the thick of it with his car. Despite the talk of MG, Austin-Healey, Jaguar, Porsche, Alfa-Romeo, and others, it was Triumph that still held the greatest allure for me. The first book I bought and read again and again was Graham Robson's 1973 *Story of Triumph Sports Cars*.

Sure, Dad's stories helped bias me but Triumph had much to boast about in those early days: racing success at Le Mans, rally success at Monte Carlo and around the world, the first manufacturer with a production car capable of 100 mph, and the first to offer disc brakes as standard equipment.

Dad was my poet laureate of the sports car invasion with his TR3. He could wax nostalgic about those early days and there was something magical to me about all of it. You will not be surprised to learn that my first car was a Triumph. A faded, 1970 Damson Red Spitfire Mark 3 replete with rusted rocker panels and a worn-out lump that burned more oil than gas. But I was not deterred in my quest to live my own version of the glory days. Engine pulled and rebuilt, rockers filled with Bondo, and off I went. Sadly, my limited high school budget prevented me from fully realizing my own version of sports car glory, but that is what inspired this book.

Looking at the history today, there isn't a Triumph enthusiast who doesn't know these things. But despite all those successes, Triumph has become a forgotten marque in the landscape of 1950s and 1960s sports cars. MG has become the ubiquitous British sports car because, let's face it, they stamped out a lot of cars. This is validated every time someone drives a TR3 and people ask "Is that an MG?" This is almost understandable because the car has no markings and the nose badge was small with only "TR" at the bottom of the shield. Some people even thought the car was an "Undo" because of the script on the wheel knock-offs.

The shorter-lived Austin-Healeys, particularly the Big Healeys, are fetching large sums at auction these days. And the sexy lines, luxurious appointments, and twin-cam V-12s have pushed Jaguar to legend status. So what happened to Triumph, which once dominated sales over all of them?

I'll be honest and tell you that my bias going into this project was for the early cars. The TR2 through TR6, and particularly the TR2, TR3, and TR4. That prejudice changed dramatically in the writing of this book. I have found a new appreciation for the GT6 and the Wedge cars that punctuated Triumph's production run.

Triumph built as many family cars as sports car between 1923 and 1982, but this book is dedicated to the sports cars: those handsome, sometimes "hairy-chested," brutes known as TRs and their cousins, Spitfire and GT6. I give you some of the background and back-office dealings that shaped Triumph's history, but stories of meetings, mergers, and financial tomfoolery, while integral to the story, are not nearly as exciting as the cars.

Triumph was a company that knew that its road car sales could be built through racing success. In fact, it was the cornerstone of its marketing platform throughout the run of TRs. Therefore, I examine the factory endurance racing and rallying efforts. Amazingly, throughout its history, Triumph also had a number of near misses that, had things gone right, could have substantially altered the fortunes of the company. Just when a groundbreaking model was on the boards, it was thwarted and the company seemed to race from one financial disaster to the next. Regardless, the cars that it did build were also unique, historic, and groundbreaking. In fact, some of Triumph's innovations endure today in other designs or marques.

It is a great history; I hope you enjoy the ride.

To finish that story I started: the 1956 TR3 was pulled from its resting place at the back of the garage and underwent a multi-year restoration. Today, it is running around Southwest Florida and was recently awarded Gold status by the Vintage Triumph Register.

CHAPTER 1
SIEGFRIED BETTMANN AND A MOTORIZED BICYCLE

Triumph's first motorized vehicle was created in 1902 when a 2¼-hp Minerva engine from Belgium was fitted into a reinforced bicycle frame. Siegfried Bettmann also experimented with a variety of power units before creating his own 5-hp units in 1905. Throughout the early part of the century, Triumph motorcycles looked similar to this 1909 version. The bicycle origins are clearly evident with the pedal chain drive and the belt drive. Triumph was known for quality and excellence, which can be seen in all of the controls, fittings, and fuel lines. (Photo Courtesy Geert Versleyen/Yesterdays Antique Motorcycles)

Triumph's automotive history does not begin with a car or even a pre-turn-of-the-century cycle car. In fact Triumph's genealogy did not even start with a motorized vehicle. The first automobile came about late in the company's timeline, some 38 years after the company's founding. But the pre-history of the car deserves some attention because of its evolution and the equally famous cycle company of the same name. Yes, they are related.

The birth of the marque dates back to the 19th Century and a transplanted German living in London. Siegfried Bettmann started his no-name bicycle business in London in 1885. A few years later, he moved his facility 100 miles northwest of the city to Coventry. It is doubtful that Bettmann foresaw Coventry as the home to as many as 20 different carmakers 50 years down the road.

In the 1890s, all sorts of experimentation was being conducted about how a person could travel faster than on foot. Bicycles were the newest and most popular form of travel and the bicycle business was therefore booming. Bettmann's brand-less bikes were enjoying brisk sales both domestically and internationally. Bettmann knew that he needed a name that would translate all over the world to ensure success so he chose the name Triumph. And thus the marque was born.

The company continued to prosper until the turn of the century when the market became saturated and the frenzied popularity of bicycles had begun to wane. Bettmann was looking for an innovation to keep his Triumph company going. He only needed to look as far as his closest competitors.

TRIUMPH'S FIRST MOTORIZED VEHICLE

At that time, most of Bettmann's competitors were experimenting with mounting small internal combustion engines on their bicycles. Adding an engine to a Triumph was as inevitable as it was natural.

In 1902, a Belgian Minerva 2.25-hp engine was fitted to a reinforced Triumph bicycle frame. This experimental unit was effectively the first Triumph motorcycle. The little Minerva was successful at propelling the bicycle, but Bettmann had plenty of other engines to test, including the locally sourced J. A. Prestwich (known today as JAP) 3-bhp units. A good engineer is always looking for more power.

After years of experimenting with JAP and a variety of other off-the-shelf engines, Triumph finally developed its own 3-hp powerplant in 1905. The new 300-cc, side-valve engines were capable of cruising at a very respectable 30 mph and sold for a not insignificant £45. It was a reasonable price for the day but edged toward expensive. This was when things really began to take off for Triumph. In 1906, the company produced slightly more than 550 motorcycles; by 1909, the company was producing 3,000 motorcycles annually.

STANDARD MOTOR COMPANY IS BORN

As the new Triumph motorcycles were enjoying this early success, it is important to note some of the other names and developments in Coventry at the time. In early 1903, Reginald Maudslay founded the Standard Motor Company; he was hard at work on his first car, the Victoria. Maudslay began the company with the idea that all parts for all cars would be interchangeable, hence the sensible name "Standard." Rapid growth and heavy competition caused this charter to be dropped, but the cars continued to be built under the Standard name. Just as the first motorcycles were motorized bicycles, the first cars were essentially motorized horse carriages. Standards were available as either open or closed models.

Standard's engineering reputation grew quickly and by 1906 it had joined the ranks of Rolls-Royce and Napier as the only manufacturers producing a 6-cylinder engine. The 1910 line of Standard coupes and saloons was considered as elegant and fashionable as the higher-ranking competition from Rolls-Royce and others.

Like Maudslay, Bettmann had also built a reputation for high quality and craftsmanship, thanks to his Triumph motorcycles. The adoring public called the motorcycles "frisky" because of their performance. Bettmann also enjoyed great personal prosperity and popularity in that period; he was elected mayor of Coventry, an odd office to be held by a German, especially in 1913. However, more important to his story is his first involvement with automobiles, which began a year earlier.

In 1912, Maudslay needed cash to buy out his partner and keep the Standard Motor Company running. Bettmann was among those offering capital. From 1912 until the outbreak of World War I in 1914, Bettmann was Chairman of the Standard Motor Company while also maintaining his leadership role at Triumph.

The war helped to further cement Triumph's reputation for quality and reliability. Approximately 30,000 of the 550-cc motorcycles were shipped to France during the war and by the end of hostilities, the military referred to them as "Trusty Triumphs." By 1920, Bettmann's motorcycles were the most popular motorbikes in Great Britain.

By this point, nearly all of Triumph's two-wheeled competitors had begun experimenting with four wheels. William Morris, also of Coventry, began building bicycles and motorcycles in 1901. By 1912, he had introduced his first car, the Morris Oxford. In 1914, the Morris Chummy debuted; it was very well received with good reviews and brisk sales. Others, including Austin, Singer, Standard, and Crosley, had evolved in a similar manner and were riding the wave of these popular new little, or "light" cars, as they were known.

TRIUMPH'S FIRST CAR

Bettmann had no choice but to follow suit. In 1921, Triumph acquired the Dawson Car Company and announced plans to produce the first Triumph automobile. Because this development was fully expected and anticipated, the announcement went virtually unnoticed by the newspapers or public. It was only a matter of when the car would be announced.

Finally, in 1923, Triumph debuted its first car called the 10/20, which was named for its Royal Automobile Club (RAC) horsepower rating of 10 and its actual horsepower of 20. The 102-inch wheelbase was nearly 20 inches longer than the other "light" cars of 1916 but was right in line with its postwar contemporaries. It was powered by a 1,393-cc 4-cylinder side-valve engine capable of 45 mph. Three body styles were available: two-seat and four-seat standard bodies and a four-seat Weymann sedan. Each was set on a typical box frame with semi-elliptic leaf springs placed

Triumph debuted its first four-wheeled vehicle in 1923. The model 10/20 was named for its Royal Automobile Club (RAC) horsepower rating of 10 and actual horsepower output of 20. The 1,393-cc 4-cylinder engine was capable of propeling the car to a top speed of 45 mph. Brakes were fitted to the rear wheels only. The high quality of fit and finish set the Triumph cars apart from the others of the day. (Photo Courtesy British Motor Industry Heritage Trust)

longitudinally front and rear. The 10/20 stood on 21-inch tires mounted on 10-spoke steel rims that were just 3⅕ inches wide.

Triumph did not set any design trends with the first car; most cars of the period looked very similar. The difference was in the final product. All of the cars were finished to the same high-quality standards as its motorcycles and aimed at the upmarket consumer who would be attracted to a car that was a level above Morris and Austin. As with the motorcycles, the cars had brakes on the rear wheels only.

The two- and four-seat bodies were priced at £430 and the Weymann body was priced at £460, which was twice that of the Morris and Austin cars. The Standard Nine models were priced at £250.

Despite rave reviews for the new Triumph cars, sales were sluggish.

In 1928, Triumph introduced the 13/30 and, one year later, its successor, the 15. Each model was larger than its predecessor in every way. The wheelbase had grown to 112 inches, the engine to 2 liters, and speeds to 55 mph. Triumph's same high standards of quality prevailed, and that drove the price up to £500. However, the cars received even less notice than the original 10/20. These cars' only claim to fame was that their hydraulic brakes were fitted to all four wheels while other cars still had two-wheel braking. Fortunately, Triumphs had at least caught on in Australia, and the motorcycles continued to sell well enough to keep the company afloat.

Meanwhile, across town at Standard, the co-founder of the Swallow Sidecar and Coachbuilding Company came calling. A young William Lyons was in the market for a chassis to fit his new car design. Lyons and partner William Walmsley had a successful business building stylish sidecars to bolt onto just about any type of motorcycle. Swallow had begun to dabble in automobiles two years earlier with its version of the Austin 7, called appropriately the Austin Seven Swallow.

Lyons, armed with a sketch penned by coachbuilder Cyril Holland, wanted to create a two-seat open car. He purchased the Standard Nine chassis, and in 1929, the Standard-Swallow debuted at £235.

The diminutive 1929 Austin Seven Swallow, with its narrow track and slightly cartoonish lines (by today's standards), was designed by the up-and-coming William Lyons of the Swallow Sidecar Company. The car was the result of Lyons' body design being mounted atop a purchased Standard Nine chassis. It was offered as a coupe and a roadster, the latter having a rather bulbous tail section. (Photo Courtesy Richard Spiegelman)

CHAPTER 1: Siegfried Bettmann and a Motorized Bicycle

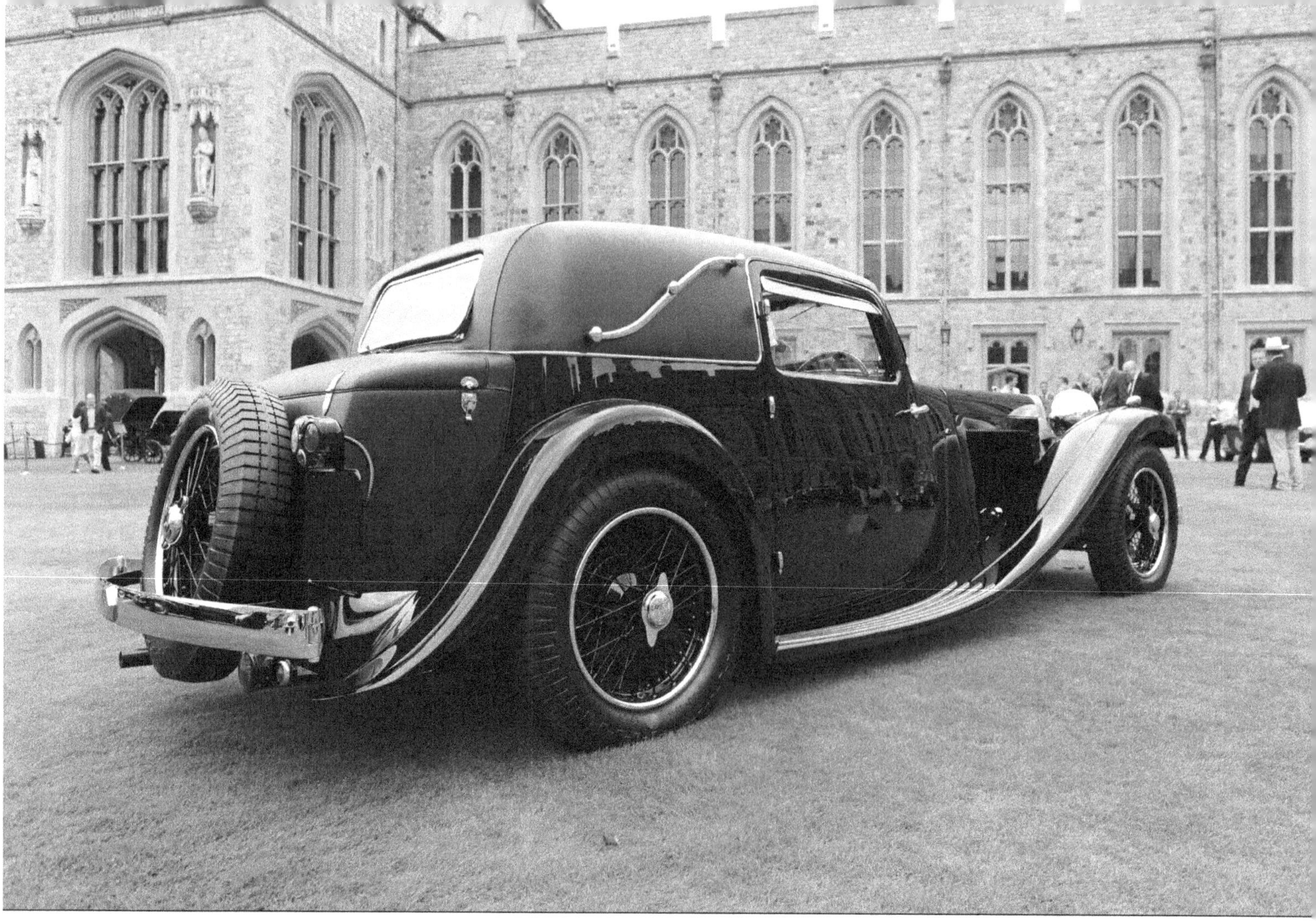

The dramatic and stylish 1933 Standard Swallow, which was later known as the SS1. In four short years, Lyons' designs had graduated from spindly little cars for everyman to the big leagues of cars with remarkable style and performance. This coupe, known as a saloon, was powered by the Standard 6-cylinder engine that made 48 hp. (Photo Courtesy Gary Harmon)

As you would expect for a car with these looks on the outside, the interior of the SS1 was spacious and well appointed. It was a very large two-passenger car, as was the trend of the day. (Photo Courtesy Gary Harmon)

Maudslay's new partner at Standard, John Black, recognized the importance of such a relationship and nurtured it along with other similar opportunities. Standard Motor Company supplied Lyons with engines and chassis to fit Swallow bodies.

Black was also instrumental in helping Lyons realize his dream of producing a distinctive new sports car. In 1933, Lyons introduced the sleek and stylish SS (formerly Standard-Swallow) sports car. This was a true roadster with its cut doors, boat tail rear, and rakish design; it looked as if it were built to go fast.

The immediate success of the new SS was the springboard from which Lyons created SS Cars Ltd. and eventually Jaguar. Of course, the Swallow name reverted to Triumph 20 years later.

As Lyons was getting started, Bettmann needed to react quickly to the slumping sales of his Triumph automobiles so he turned his attention to "light" cars. As with the pre-war cars, these were essentially identical to the current

The popular 1932 Super Nine four-door sedan. These smart-looking saloons exhibited Triumph's reputation for quality fit and finish and, along with its performance, helped pave the way toward Triumph's first official sports car: the Gloria Southern Cross. The most prominent feature of the car was the 1,018-cc 9-hp Coventry Climax i.o.e. (inlet over exhaust) engine. With the exhaust valves on the side, pushrod-actuated intake valves over the top, and fed by a Solex carburetor, the car could achieve a top speed of 50 mph. An uprated 1,122-cc version of the engine delivered 10 hp and an additional 15 mph in the Southern Cross. Triumph sourced engines from Coventry Climax from the end of the Great Depression until the late 1930s when the company began building its own engines. (Photo Courtesy Simon Goldsworthy/*Triumph World*)

production cars but of a smaller scale, almost like shrunken kiddy cars for adults. However, Bettmann was determined to maintain the same high quality of his full-sized line.

In the fall of 1927, Triumph introduced "the last word in the smallest class," the Super Seven. Whether it was premonition, foresight, or just plain luck on the part of Bettmann, it proved to be the car that established Triumph as a prominent auto manufacturer.

The new little car had a wheelbase of just 81 inches and a width of 51 inches but it had room for four adults. It was powered by a 21-hp 832-cc 4-cylinder capable of 48 mph. The ladder frame featured semi-elliptic springs at the front, shock absorbers at all four wheels, and Lockheed hydraulic brakes. The customer had a choice of 19-inch 10-spoke stamped steel wheels or the more-sporting wire wheels. A bare chassis could be purchased for just £113 and a completed car for only £149.

This pricing made the car popular among coachbuilders as well as the public. At £149, the Super Seven cost more than the very popular Austin Chummy (£135) and the Singer 8 (£140), but Triumph was able to promote its higher level of quality as well as advanced comfort and safety features.

By 1928, Triumph was offering the Super Seven in six body styles ranging in price from £149 to £200. The most expensive was a custom-bodied sedan complete with leather interior. Prominent coachbuilders shied away from little cars. However, the Triumphs were so versatile that revered names such as Morgan-Hastings created cars on the Seven chassis.

SUPER SEVEN AND DONALD HEALEY

Bettmann was only concerned with his cars' successes on the showroom floor; he paid little attention to the fact that the Seven was also enjoying competition success. By winning countless speed and endurance challenges across Australia and in the United Kingdom, the little Triumphs were building a reputation as sports cars. Of particular note is the name of one of the most successful drivers, Donald Healey, who later joined the company as Experimental Manager in 1934.

The success of the Super Seven continued through 1932, when it moved upscale with nicer appointments and became the Super Eight. In 1932, the Super Nine was also introduced; it boasted a new Coventry Climax 1-liter engine capable of 60 mph. Triumph was one of a handful of car manufacturers to survive the Great Depression, during which scores had failed. Lacking funds to design and build a new 4-cylinder engine, it sourced powerplants from Coventry Climax, located just a mile down the road.

With this car Triumph formally recognized the sports car market with a new body design called Southern Cross. It was an open car featuring a fold-down windshield, wire wheels, and semi-cut-down doors. Under the narrow hood sat a bored-out version of the Climax engine. It was a bit awkward and looked disproportionate, as did all the Seven models because of their short wheelbase. The Southern Cross received its wings when it was made part of the larger Gloria line in 1935.

The Gloria line of cars was actually quite stylish and attractive at the time. The cars were powered by 1,087- or 1,232-cc 4-cylinders engines or the optional 1,467- or 1,991-cc 6-cylinder Coventry Climax engines. The I Gloria Tourer looked a bit gangly because of the long wheelbase and this was particularly so with the softtop in place.

To create the sporting two-seat Southern Cross, the wheelbase was cut by a full 12 inches. The lines may not have flowed well, but it was certainly sporty and aggressive looking. Imagine, if you will, a more brutish version of the T-series MG with the notched doors. They were not fully cut-down doors because the downward angle rose again to meet the rear of the car, which appeared more rugged because of the external fuel tank sandwiched between the cockpit and the dual spare tires.

But credit is due to Donald Healey for making this 1,232-cc-powered underslung car into a sporting success. His Monte Carlo version featured dual down-draft Zenith carburetors delivering 48 bhp.

From 1934 to 1938 Triumph had a successful run of cars based on the Gloria platform. The platform allowed a variety of bodies to be almost interchangeable on the Super Nine chassis. All models featured conventional semi-elliptic leaf springs on all four corners, along with hydraulic brakes. (Photo Courtesy Simon Goldsworthy/*Triumph World*)

The Gloria line featured coupes, open two-seater roadsters, and larger enclosed touring models. This sporting two-seater Southern Cross, named for the constellation, was the result of shortening the 108-inch wheelbase by 12 inches. This created a sportier and more proportional-looking car. The Monte Carlo version used this same cut-door design but the additional length made it less proportional in profile. (Photo Courtesy Simon Goldsworthy/*Triumph World*)

The cut-down doors were a common styling element at the time. However, Triumph trademarked an optional hinged flip-up panel to fill in the gap in inclement weather. (Photo Courtesy Simon Goldsworthy/*Triumph World*)

This 1,232-cc engine is fitted with dual side-draft carburetors. Donald Healey went on to fit larger 30-mm Zenith down-draft carburetors that boosted horsepower to 48 for competition. (Photo Courtesy Simon Goldsworthy/*Triumph World*)

The remarkable 1934 Dolomite Straight Eight. Named for the Italian mountain range, the car was inspired by Alfa-Romeo's world-beating 8C; it is sometimes referred to as Triumph 8C. When the car was in development, Donald Healey traveled to Italy to meet the designers of the Alfa to ensure he got all the details right. A U.S.-based car collector, who owns several Alfa 8Cs and one of the surviving Dolomites, said that, in his experience, the Triumph was quicker and handled better than its Italian inspiration. (Photo Courtesy Gary Harman)

The arresting lines of the Dolomite Straight Eight were designed by Walter Belgrove. The body sat on a pressed-steel ladder frame supported by semi-elliptic leaf springs at all four corners. (Photo Courtesy Gary Harman)

CHAPTER 1: Siegfried Bettmann and a Motorized Bicycle

As this was all happening, Bettmann had had enough and retired. Claude Holbrook replaced him. The new management faced great challenges during the early 1930s. The light-car boom was over; Gloria sedans and saloons were not selling, but production costs were rising quickly. Only the motorcycles continued to thrive.

During this same period, Healey proposed and built Triumph's first great car, and perhaps its greatest. He was fresh from his success at the Alpine Trial with a bare-bones Southern Cross Monte Carlo that had dominated the competition. He wanted to build a car capable of challenging the big names from Germany and Italy.

Healey's creation was the Dolomite Straight Eight, which was modeled directly from the highly successful Alfa-Romeo 2300. In fact, not only did Healey purchase an Alfa for research, he also traveled to Italy to speak directly to the car's designers to be certain he got it as correct as possible.

THE REMARKABLE DOLOMITE STRAIGHT EIGHT

Triumph's new car, named for the famed mountain range, was like no other it had built before or since. This project was both a brilliant engineering feat and a miraculous financial feat because the company was seriously strapped for cash. This was, unfortunately, a recurring theme throughout Triumph's history. It was perennially short of financial resources just as it was on the verge of creating a car that could have completely changed the fortunes of the company. The Dolomite was the first of several very special cars.

Looking similar to the Alfa, it featured a hand-built 1,990-cc double overhead cam (DOHC) 8-cylinder engine boasting 120 hp aided by a Roots supercharger. The engine's design almost made it appear as if two 4-cylinder engines had been fused inline. This appearance was accentuated by the dual four-pipe intake manifolds feeding each cylinder from two Zenith down-draft carburetors. On the opposite side of the engine were eight individual exhaust pipes that curved down and out through an opening in the hood in the style of the Frazer-Nash. The eight pipes joined a single large muffler running longitudinally just ahead of the passenger-side door. The exhaust was then piped to the rear of the car.

Power was channeled to the rear wheels through an Armstrong Siddeley-Wilson pre-selector gearbox sourced from Siddeley. Pre-selector gearboxes were in vogue at the time, but usually only found in the upper end of the automobile spectrum on vehicles such as Mercedes-Benz, Bugatti, Maybach, and Talbot-Lago.

A pre-selector gearbox was preferred in the Dolomite because it allowed for fast and easy shifting. However, more important was the fact that it could handle more power than a conventional manual transmission.

Named in part for Major W. G. Wilson, one of the co-inventors of the tank during World War I, the transmission had many internal operational similarities to an automatic transmission. The driver could select a gear ahead of time on the small mechanism tucked neatly within a finger's reach behind the steering wheel. When the gear change was required, the driver simply pressed and released the gear change pedal (similar to a clutch pedal) and the new gear was engaged. It was quick with no possibility of a missed shift and the driver's hands remained on the steering wheel.

This on-the-street snapshot captures Donald Healey showing the Straight Eight engine compartment to a group of inquisitive young men while stopped during a road test. The photo is thought to have been taken in Perranporth, Cornwall. (Photo Courtesy Rich Saunders)

The heart of the beast: the hand-built DOHC 1,990-cc inline 8-cylinder engine. With the help of a Roots supercharger, horsepower was rated at 120 bhp and capable of top speeds more than 110 mph. Looking like two 4-cylinder engines fused together, it was actually one alloy block with alloy head that featured 10 main bearings. (Photo Courtesy Simon Goldsworthy/*Triumph World*)

The multi-plate dry clutch was set to engage at a relatively low RPM when compared to competition cars with a similar setup. This made the car more street-able in town. Touring cars equipped with the pre-selector gearbox favored the fluid flywheel clutch, which was closer in feel to an automatic.

The Dolomite sat on semi-elliptic longitudinal leaf springs and Rudge-Whitworth 19-inch wire wheels. The 120 horses were harnessed by 12-inch Lockheed hydraulic brakes at all four wheels. Walter Belgrove designed the

This is the driver's view of the instruments for the Straight Eight. The control for the Wilson pre-selector gearbox can be seen to the right of the steering wheel. The driver could change gears easily by moving the lever into position and then simply dipping the clutch at the appropriate time. Gearboxes of this type were typically found on the mightier European marques such as Mercedes-Benz and Maybach. (Photo Courtesy Gary Harman)

Although Donald Healey's amazing Straight Eight Dolomite did not go into production, he was instrumental in the engine changes for the Dolomite saloons and roadsters offered from 1937 to 1939. He converted all Climax engines to overhead-valve configuration for greater efficiency and reliability. Walter Belgrove penned the fashionable body lines, which can be likened to the Jaguar and MG saloons of the day. However, the distinctive "waterfall" grilles with bounteous rounded chrome was not popular. (Photo Courtesy Simon Goldsworthy/*Triumph World*)

body for the purposeful-looking open two-seater. It was, and still is, a very stylish design.

Healey's work was pure genius. Everything in the Dolomite was built in the Coventry facility by Healey and his crew. They undoubtedly racked up some hefty overtime hours because the car was completed in just six months.

The car performed brilliantly in almost every test, with the straight-8 capable of sustaining 100 mph (and faster) and could run the quarter-mile in 17.8 seconds. In an interview with *Motor Sport* magazine, Healey said he was disappointed that the car fell short of the 120 mph he had hoped for on a lap at Brooklands.

Nevertheless, Healey was highly encouraged by the Dolomite's performance and entered the 1935 Monte Carlo rally. Healey was well acquainted with the event and had won the 1931 rally in an Invicta. His new Triumph looked poised for a top finish.

Car No. 1 was rebuilt on an even tighter budget to run again in the 1936 Monte Carlo rally. Healey finished eighth, running the entire event without the aid of the supercharger. All indications are that the Dolomite was every bit a match for the Alfa-Romeo 2300. However, fate intervened. It was to be the last glory savored by Triumph; the fortunes of the company were about to change permanently.

The motorcycle division was sold off that year to raise cash, and the Dolomite program was canceled with only three cars built. The Dolomite name was migrated to a new line of production sedans set to bow in the next year.

It is unfortunate that the Dolomite did not survive the accountant's guillotine because a line of exclusive and exotic cars with the kind of performance pedigree Healey engineered could have set Triumph on a very different course.

TRIUMPH FALLS ON HARD TIMES

Times were tight and more changes came at the top. Holbrook was replaced by one of his old rallying partners, Maurice Newnham. However, Newnham had developed a bent for family cars and by 1937, the only sporting production car in the Triumph lineup was the Southern Cross. Its "sporting" nature was rather limited because it was only available with a 4-cylinder engine of modest performance.

A series of unremarkable sedans and saloons that blended into the background of Rileys, MGs, and Austins followed. They were good cars to be sure, with a reputation for being big and slow but possessing no sporting flair. Newnham took a lot of flack for fitting the 1937 Dolomite coupes and saloons with an obnoxiously large, chrome nose with the hope of attracting the American market. It failed miserably and Triumph's fortunes declined further.

By 1939 only 50 cars were built, and Triumph Motor Company was put on the auction block. Bidding for the troubled car manufacturer was just as underwhelming as unit sales. Eventually, steel manufacturer Thomas Ward took the helm of Triumph just as war was declared on Germany. The Coventry factory was closed for the duration.

Ward kept Donald Healey on as general manager to help sell the company. Unfortunately, while Healey was presenting the company to potential suitors as a viable operation in need of financial support, Ward was selling off many of Triumph's manufacturing assets. This left little to interest any potential buyer.

Healey had his own vision for Triumph after the war. He presented a design for a new line of sports cars to Ward and his board of directors. Unfortunately, the ideas were rejected so Ward continued with the sale of the company.

During the 1930s and 1940s, many carmakers were absorbed by larger entities or simply faded from existence. It's a bit of a miracle that the Triumph badge carried on. Credit lucky timing and the war.

This is also where Healey's involvement with Triumph ends. He took his ideas across town to Riley, which was interested in working with him. It began to build the Healey car in 1946 and everyone knows where that led. It was another great one that got away from Triumph.

As hostilities wound down and peacetime manufacturing resumed, only a few logical buyers for Triumph were revealed: Austin, Rootes, and Standard. Austin didn't need Triumph; it would have fit better with Rootes' marques Sunbeam and Hillman. Standard made the most sense.

Standard was thriving with an output of 50,000 cars in 1939 and looking to expand under newly appointed managing director John Black. He had recognized the dangers of events in Germany well before war was declared. He had begun working with the British government and preparing to convert factories for wartime production.

By doing so, Black was able to keep his company running during the war years. Standard built primarily armored cars, but its most significant contribution was production of the all-wooden Mosquito fighter/bomber.

Black was instrumental in keeping manufacturing plants running to support the war effort in Britain. As a result, he was knighted after the end of World War II.

Just as Black was savvy enough to anticipate the declaration of war, he also saw it drawing to a close. Before the last shot was fired, Standard was already converting factories back to auto production. That's when John Black went in search of a sports car to complement his line of family cars.

CHAPTER 2

TRIUMPH'S FIRST SPORTS CAR

The acerbic Sir John Black. His leadership and efforts during World War II resulted in his knighthood, but he was known for being a harsh taskmaster. Wise and forward thinking in many ways, Black was also capable of making important decisions based solely on emotion. He is seen here with the first Mayflower two-door coupe, another project he oversaw personally. (Photo Courtesy British Motor Industry Heritage Trust)

The T-series MGs are most frequently credited as being the catalyst for the sports car invasion of the United States. Returning U.S. servicemen brought home more than the spoils of war, they brought back unique little cars. The sporty little MG TA two-seaters with narrow track and skinny wire wheels were like nothing else on American roads of the day. People clamored to get one. And MG's place became firmly entrenched in automobile lore. The Triumph story is not so quaint or romantic.

To say that nothing was left of Triumph at the end of the war is a gross understatement. Even if German bombs had not reduced the Briton Road factory to rubble, there would have been no way to build a car because Ward sold off all tooling and production facilities. Triumph had also lost Healey's deft touch for sports car design after he left to pursue his ideas for his own car. John Black had nothing left but a small cache of replacement parts and barely usable engineering drawings. Fortunately, Black still had William Lyons.

What cannot be glossed over here is the marvel of how quickly companies such as Standard got back to the business of building cars after the end of the war. It was not just that they had stopped building cars in favor of aircraft or tanks, the factories were bombed heavily and repeatedly. Imagine 1940s Detroit being bombed regularly for years and then to begin retooling for car manufacturing in a mere few months.

As the war drew to a close in 1944, Lyons went right back to work building his cars. However, he dropped "SS" from the company name because of the very unfortunate link to the German military unit. In 1939, Standard began supplying Lyons' SS-Jaguar company with an ever-growing number of engines, gearboxes, and axles. Standard also picked up where it had left off. At the time, Black's personal car happened to be an SS100. Probably not a conflict of interest but it may have raised a few eyebrows.

It was clear to see how many engines were going to Jaguar. Therefore, Black, who was known to be a harsh taskmaster and also to make emotional decisions, decided that he wanted to add a sporting image to Standard. It was the obvious move after he had made an attempt to partner with Lyons' company but was rejected on the spot. Reacting impulsively, Black offered to sell Lyons the remaining 6-cylinder engines and all the associated tooling. Lyons seized the opportunity and with one fell swoop gathered everything up and skedaddled down the road before Black could back out. From this day forward, Black was determined to beat Lyons at his own game; he wanted a sports car that would compete with and beat Jaguar head-on.

In 1944, Standard purchased what remained of Triumph for £75,000. It then promptly sold the remains of the factory for the same amount but kept just the name Triumph, essentially for free. At that point, it was unclear what was to become of it.

It should be noted that at this point in the chronology, the charismatic tractor builder Harry Ferguson arrived on the scene. He was looking to establish his tractors in England and needed manufacturing space. Black had a vast production facility left over from the war that he needed to fill so they formed an alliance.

Black, already anticipating the conclusion of the war, badly wanted to be the first car manufacturer back in full production. In 1944, he authorized the beginning of new body designs for Standard. Because it was going to take all hands to get the new Standard models up to speed, Black decided that he would oversee the design and production of the new sports car personally. The new car was going to be produced under the Triumph banner. It would begin as his own personal car and that would eventually become the production model.

At this point, all Black had was the Triumph nameplate, which had a history and reputation for quality. It should be noted that Triumph had enjoyed a higher reputation for quality than Standard, so Black had a good base from which to start. But, he had no experienced designers, no chassis, and Lyons had taken his 6-cylinder engines. At one point, Black even tried to hire Cecil Kimber to run the new venture and develop the new sports car. Kimber, the man behind MG's pre-war success, declined the offer just days before a freak rail accident at King's Cross Station in London took his life.

Sir John Black (seated) and Harry Ferguson (second from left) formed an alliance wherein Triumph supplied the Vanguard 4-cylinder wet-sleeve engines for Ferguson tractor manufacture in England. The TE20 tractors, known as "Fergies" were built in excess Triumph manufacturing space at Banner Lane. This partnership provided Triumph with much-needed capital for development of new cars. Black's eventual successor, Alick Dick, can be seen behind his right shoulder. (Photo Courtesy British Motor Industry Heritage Trust)

Sir John Black wanted Triumph's new post-war sports car to be modeled after the Jaguar SS100. Black's own personal car was an SS100 and he charged two fledgling designers with the task of creating the new car. (Photo Courtesy Richard Spiegelman)

THE FIRST POST-WAR SPORTS CAR

It was determined that there would be two new Triumph models: a saloon and an open touring roadster. The cars would be manufactured using the knowledge gained from building aircraft, which included using tubular frames and aluminum bodywork. However, there was virtually no budget, so Black had to settle for using existing Standard components as much as possible.

Black charged two fresh, young draftsmen, Frank Callaby and Arthur Ballard, to come up with a roadster as sleek and stylish as the SS100. In 1946, Frank Callaby penned a design that became the first post-war car to carry the Triumph badge: the 1800 Roadster. The design of the car has been credited primarily to Callaby, although writings indicate that Callaby's greatest influence was on the front of the car while Ballard concentrated on the rear.

The new car was built using the skills learned from years of wartime manufacturing, specifically in building the center fuselage for the Mosquito fighter. The frame for the 1800 was built from tubular steel, which would have been easy enough given the experience level, but the challenge was that it had to be easily modified to support the saloon. The idea was to use a shorter frame for the sports car but a longer frame for the family car.

The body would be hand-formed aluminum wrapped around an ash wood frame. At the time, this was typical for most British manufacturers. Ash frame components were used famously in Morgan cars as well for decades to come.

The styling of the car was as unusual as some of its features. It bore no resemblance to any of Triumph's contemporaries, and certainly no likeness to Black's SS100. The similarities might have been in spirit but were certainly not physical.

Starting at the front, from a head-on view, the car was impressive and slightly imposing. With its tall grille, massive chrome headlamps, and dual horns, it looked like a descendant of the 1930s classic era. However, its profile did not harken to the same classics.

The rear track of the car was 5 inches wider (12.7 cm) than the front track (presumably to gain more passenger room) so the car was at a proportional disadvantage immediately.

Triumph's first post-war sports car and the first car to carry the Triumph badge after World War II. Frank Callaby and Arthur Ballad designed the 1800 Roadster and modeled it from the Jaguar SS100. The styling represents a 10-year evolution from the SS100 of the mid-1930s to the post-war trend toward fully enveloped bodies. (Photo Courtesy Warwick Carter)

The 1800 Roadster shows some disproportions, likely caused by the two designers splitting duty between the front and rear of the car. The long hood and statuesque grille are reminiscent of a pre-war Jaguar, but aft of the windshield post the car becomes compressed and quickly curtailed. It is an open car and named a "Roadster," but it is not a roadster in the same sense as other sports cars of the day. (Photo Courtesy Warwick Carter)

The tall and imposing grille, large close-mounted headlamps, and dual horns harkened back to the pre-war classics. The body of the Roadsters were assembled in the Canley factory using pre-war methods with aluminum panels formed on the same presses that once produced aircraft fuselages. The manual construction process limited output to just over 2,500 of the 1800 Roadsters produced. (Photo Courtesy Warwick Carter)

Triumph maintained its pre-war reputation for quality with the interior. The plush interior featured a polished walnut veneer dashboard, roll-up windows, and padded door panels. Marketing materials claimed that the cockpit could seat three adults. Given that the full width of the car was just 64 inches, it was an optimistic claim. (Photo Courtesy Warwick Carter)

The long, narrow hood was flanked by rounded bulbous, pontoon-like fenders. Unlike the more sleek motorcycle-style fenders of the Jaguar and MG T-series, the hand-beaten front fenders were freestanding but were fared into the body ahead of the doors. The fenders virtually enveloped the front wheels from front to rear with a demure running light mounted at the top. Sandwiched between the end of the front fender and the start of the rear wheel arch were smallish doors that were hinged at the rear. The flip-out metal trafficator was fared-in just behind the door hinge.

From the rear wheel arch to the grille, the car was stylish and handsome. Looking rearward from the doors is where things became somewhat disproportioned. In relation to the long hood, the car ended quickly with the high, rounded trunk dropping off almost immediately aft of the axle.

Seating was by far the most unique feature of the car. An American-style bench seat filled the two-door cockpit and *claimed* to fit three adults. The plush interior was of high-quality fit and finish that featured an all-wood dash, two-spoke steering wheel, roll-up windows, and padded door panels with wood trim. These were all quality hallmarks of the original Triumph badge.

A curious addition was a hideaway seat in the style of an American rumble seat, or British dickie seat, that opened like a clam shell from the rear deck with two individually folding seatbacks. Unlike American rumble seats, the assembly included a stout flip-up windscreen that was similar to pre-war dual-cowl phaetons. Black frequently contributed to designs in an effort to be like Lyons, and the unique rear seat was said to be his idea, or rather, his insistence.

The auxiliary seating at the rear of the car was the Roadster's most unique feature and provided space for two additional passengers. Known as a dickie seat, the apparatus is simple to operate. Turn the handle to roll the rear hatch back into place and flip up the secondary windscreen. When the seat assembly is closed, the foot well doubles as a parcel compartment. However, anything placed in this space can be viewed easily through the folded-down windscreen because it becomes part of the body form when closed. (Photo Courtesy Warwick Carter)

Most adults would likely find it difficult to climb into the supplemental seating compartment. Although there are steps, small rubber pads on the bumpers, there are no additional aides to getting into the compartment. Climbing around the open hatch is better suited for younger passengers. The space itself is not claustrophobic, but the seats are really only adequate for short distances. (Photo Courtesy Warwick Carter)

Climbing into the rear auxiliary seats was no easy feat. The two folding seats were adequate for short trips but would be harsh and unyielding over a long journey.

When compared to Black's target of the Jaguar SS100, the 1800 Roadster was a big car at 175 inches (444.5 cm) long, 64 inches wide (162.5 cm), and 56 inches tall (142.2 cm). The Jaguar was 153 inches (388.6 cm) long, 63 inches (160.0 cm) wide, and 52 inches tall (130.0 cm). The Jag sat two, while the 1800 advertised seating for five.

Compared to the archetype MG TC's 139.5-inch length (354.3 cm), 56-inch (142.2 cm) width, and 53-inch height (134.6 cm), the Triumph was titanic. The 1800 Roadster's aluminum bodywork atop a tubular steel chassis was a technological leap over the MG ash and plywood undercarriage. The post-war steel shortage prompted the use of aluminum bodywork, which was a blessing in disguise for Triumph. Imagine what stamped steel bodywork would have added to the car's weight!

Beneath the long hood sat the venerable 4-cylinder OHV 1,776-cc, engine. This was the same engine that Lyons had also been buying steadily from Standard. However, this engine was not part of the deal when Black impetuously sold components to Lyons.

The 4-cylinder's 63 hp was routed through the same 4-speed gearbox that was also being supplied to Jaguar.

The T-series MG is frequently credited as being the catalyst for the British sports car invasion in the years immediately following World War II. At the time, the small cars with their narrow track and very open two-seat cockpits were a true novelty on U.S. highways. The T-series had body-on-frame construction throughout the 19-year run beginning in 1936. A 1,250-cc engine making 54 hp powered the TC; just enough to start the thirst for open-air motoring. (Photo Courtesy Classic Car Garage)

The elegantly appointed Renown was among the first post-war models to carry the Triumph badge. Sharing the same platform with the Roadster, bodywork was built by Mulliners of Birmingham. Body panels were formed over a wooden buck using sheets of aluminum. Steel was still scarce after the war and aluminum was cheaper and more plentiful. Approximately 4,000 Renowns were built between 1949 and 1954. (Photo Courtesy Simon Goldsworthy/*Triumph World*)

However, the shift linkage was modified to move from a floor shift to a column shift, which became quite popular after the war. In addition, the column shift made it easier to fit a bench seat to accommodate a third passenger.

The 1800's 1,776-cc wet-sleeve engine was used through the 1948 models. In 1949 the Roadster received the 2-liter (2,088-cc) engine that boosted horsepower from 63 to 68 and delivered an additional 10 mph in top speed. (Photo Courtesy Warwick Carter)

This powerplant propelled the 1800 Roadster from 0–60 mph in a lackadaisical 34.4 seconds. While the TC was no rocket, it reached 60 mph in a more invigorating 22.7 seconds. Both were easily bested by the Jaguar's 13.5 seconds to 60 mph.

The underpinnings for the Roadster were all scavenged from Standard's pre-war parts bin. Independent front suspension was achieved via a transverse leaf spring, upper wishbones, and lever-arm shocks. Semi-elliptic leaf springs and lever-arm shocks controlled the rear with 10-inch (25.4 cm) drum brakes fitted to all four corners.

Autocar magazine tested the 1800 Roadster in 1947 and declared it to be just adequate. High marks were given to the stability and visibility, but it received very low marks for performance, particularly the vague 4-speed shifter.

The price of the Roadster was listed at £695. Not likely considered a bargain at the time, but not at the high end of the spectrum either. Unfortunately, in the immediate post-war era, raw materials were hard to come by and customers could end up waiting literally years for their new car.

The saloon that was to share the scalable tubular frame did not resemble the Roadster in any way. Looking a little like a three-quarter Bentley of the same era, it featured elegant razor-edge styling. Designed by coachbuilder Mulliners with input from Callaby, the final polish came from Walter Belgrove, who was freshly released from wartime

The Mayflower was another project driven by Sir John Black's personal oversight. The goal was to create a small saloon with razor-edge styling expressly for the U.S. market. Designed by Mulliners with stamped steel bodies built by Fisher and Ludlow, Americans found the shape to be controversial and the 38-hp side-valve engine to be underwhelming. (Photo Courtesy Simon Goldsworthy/*Triumph World*)

duties. The four-door car originally debuted as the 1800 Town and Country Saloon and saw several iterations before being renamed the Renown Saloon in 1950. It had a longer and more successful life than the Roadster.

The 1800 Roadster remained unchanged from 1946 through 1948. For 1949 the 2-liter (2,088 cc) wet-sleeve engine from the Vanguard sedan replaced the 1,776-cc unit, which boosted horsepower to 68 and gave the top speed an additional 10-mph. This was a pivotal change because the 2,088-cc "Vanguard engine" became the heart of Triumph's future sports cars.

Rewind, for a moment, back to the arrival of Harry Ferguson and his tractors. It is commonly thought that the Vanguard engine was plucked from the tractor assembly line and dropped into the Triumph. It is actually the other way around.

Ted Grinham was Standard's Technical Director at the time and in many interviews has stated that the removable, water-surrounded cylinder sleeve concept was based on a Citroën design. The engine received its name from the immensely popular Triumph Vanguard sedans. It also happened to deliver loads of torque that made it desirable for use in tractors, as Ferguson did.

From 1948 to 1950, 4,500 2000 Roadsters were produced before production was halted. Long before the last car rolled down the line, Black had abandoned his desire to

The side view of the Mayflower better illustrates the awkward lines of the car. To achieve the razor-edge styling, the Renown was used as the base, but the wheelbase was reduced by 24 inches. Although it was not a success in its intended market, the Mayflower model went on to sell more than 35,000 units in Britain and Australia. (Photo Courtesy Simon Goldsworthy/*Triumph World*)

CHAPTER 2: Triumph's First Sports Car

The Renown Saloon, which shared a platform with the Roadster, bore no resemblance to the sporting version whatsoever. This elegant four-door is also a prime example of razor-edge styling. The same 2-liter engine was shared across both body types; however, the Saloon's version had a longer production run than the Roadster. (Photo Courtesy British Motor Industry Heritage Trust)

Officially called the TR-X (for "TRiumph eXperimental") Triumph's new prototype debuted at the 1950 Paris Auto Show. The futuristic coupe was later nicknamed the "Silver Bullet" because of its double-wall aluminum envelope body and metallic-gray exterior. (Photo Courtesy Plain English)

build a Jaguar beater. A few years earlier, Lyons had upped the ante significantly when he unveiled the magnificent and gorgeous Jaguar XK120.

The astute Black had refocused his sights on the U.S. sports car market with the goal of filling the gap between the rudimentary MGs and the sophisticated Jaguars.

At the same time, Black was also personally overseeing the development of the Mayflower sedans. The two- and four-door cars also featured the razor-edge styling but with high-end features in a low-priced car. In his eyes, this car was going to be a big hit when it arrived in U.S. showrooms, hence the name Mayflower. Despite Black's best efforts (a lot of effort and money was spent), the new cars landed in 1950 with a resounding thud.

By all accounts the Mayflower was not a bad car. Fit and finish were very good and it represented a great value. Unfortunately, the love-it-or-hate-it styling was seen as quirky and the 38-hp 1,247-cc engine failed to get any attention. Consider the Mayflower alongside a 1950 Ford Crestliner with a flathead V-8. No contest.

The Experimental Sports Car

Triumph's all-new sports car, the TR-X, first appeared at the 1950 Paris auto show. Named for TRiumph eXperimental, the car was the brain-child of Walter Belgrove. A few years earlier, as the Roadster was foundering, Black launched a new sports car initiative. Belgrove was given free rein to design a sports car that would take the world by storm. The final concept was unlike anything that had been seen before and caused great controversy in the automotive press.

The TR-X, later nicknamed "Silver Bullet," was a double-wall aluminum envelope-bodied two-seater wrapped around a too-short Vanguard sedan chassis. The short wheelbase, small cockpit, and narrow track gave it a high beltline and tiny folding top. The 2,088-cc engine from the Roadster, bumped to 71 bhp, powered it with the help of larger SU carburetors. Futuristic designs were just becoming all the rage, and Belgrove's car was no exception. It looked like a 1950s concept of George Jetson's sports car from the TV cartoon show *The Jetsons*.

It was later dubbed the "push-button roadster" because it was packed with every conceivable modern luxury option, obviously aimed at Americans. It included electro-hydraulically powered seats, windows, and top, as well as hideaway headlights, inboard hydraulic jacks, a power hood that could be opened from either side, and overdrive transmission.

The motoring press either loved or deplored the car and debated about it for a year in response to Triumph's continuing publicity. It was a moot point because the TR-X never reached production. One year after its debut Black, in an attempt to save face, announced that only a limited number of TR-Xs were to be built despite the "thousands of orders" that were received. The real reasons for the delays

The two-seater later became known as the "push-button roadster" because it was loaded with every conceivable modern luxury option. Clearly aimed at the U.S. market, the car featured power seats, power windows and top, a power hood that could open from either side, and even inboard power jacks. (Photo Courtesy Plain English)

The TR-X, or "Bullet" was the first Triumph to offer hideaway headlights. The electrically controlled doors dropped into the forward portion of the fenders. Despite several other prototypes featuring hidden headlamps, it wasn't until 1975 that they were incorporated into a production model. (Photo Courtesy Moss Motors)

Walter Belgrove designed the TR-X as a replacement for the Roadster. Three prototypes were built and mounted on the Standard Vanguard chassis. Interestingly, nothing from this project carried over to the new sports cars that took the world by storm. (Photo Courtesy Plain English)

CHAPTER 2: Triumph's First Sports Car

The rear view illustrates how fully enveloped the all-aluminum body was, right down to the skirts on the rear wheels and diminutive door handles. Three working prototypes were completed but suffered from frequent system failures. It was highly ambitious and forward thinking, but it's doubtful that production versions would have been sustainable. (Photo Courtesy Moss Motors)

were Standard's lack of production capacity and capital to produce the complicated body and over-the-top options. In the end, only two examples of the car were built which, in hindsight, is fortunate. Had Standard built the car it is unlikely that the design would have held up over time because it was so out of synch with the market.

The demise of the TR-X was one-third of a triple blow to Black and Standard. Not only was he left without a sports car, but William Lyons had just brought out his enormously well-received XK120. In addition, Morgan had rejected Black's bid to acquire his company just as the promising new Plus 4 model (powered by the same Vanguard 2,088-cc engine) was coming out.

The never-say-die Sir John Black was not to be denied. He demanded that Belgrove and his designers come up with a simple, inexpensive sports car to go head-to-head with MG and Morgan. His directive dictated off-the-shelf parts, the 1,991-cc Vanguard engine, a £500 price tag, and a 90-mph top speed. The body would need to be new, but also as inexpensive as possible to produce. At the time an MG TD went for £530; £565 would buy a Morgan Plus 4. A new Donald Healey creation, the "100," was debuting at £750.

BACK TO THE DRAWING BOARD: THE FIRST TR

A prototype was built in just eight weeks and the public had its first look at the new 20TS (later known as TR1) at the Earls Court Motor Show in 1952. Reviews were mixed, but all agreed on three things: high potential performance, the striking front end and radiator opening, and something had to be done about the stubby rear end and exposed spare tire.

The simple nose with recessed radiator opening was the most popular design element of the car. This could be termed a happy accident because it was a result of cost-saving measures. A true grille would cost extra to produce, but a hole was cheap. A coarse-grate screen was eventually added to the back of the opening.

The cutaway doors (later nicknamed "kidney coolers" in some circles) were sporty (in the style of MG T-Series and Jaguar) and a cost-saving measure. Attaching the fenders with nuts and bolts was the least expensive route. The seams between the body and fenders were covered with a metal bead that was originally body color, but later changed to chrome, which gave the car a distinctive look. The no-nonsense cockpit featured two bucket seats and a full array of gauges to emphasize the seriousness of the sportiness.

The directive for a small and light car meant minimal overhang at the front and rear, which is why the tail of the car cuts off so abruptly. The exposed spare tire was an effort to blend an element of MG and Morgan into the car.

The stubby form was bolted to an out-of-the-parts-bin Standard Flying Nine chassis. The 7-foot 4-inch wheelbase was well-suited for the sports prototype, but the frame itself was limiting, to say the least. It wasn't terribly stout by sports car standards of the day and rear suspension travel was limited by the side rails. The rear axle was held in place by half-elliptic leaf springs, but the rear axle sat on top of the main frame rails. The rails limited travel severely and rendered the lever-arm shock absorbers nearly useless.

At the other end, the more modern tubular shock absorbers used in the Mayflower were the obvious choice for the front suspension. Additional reinforcements were necessary at all mounting points.

The mandated Vanguard power unit was nestled low in the front of the frame. It was counter-balanced at the rear by the fuel tank and spare tire. The 20TS had a very low center of gravity that eliminated the need for anti-roll bars. More cost savings!

Again, the cosmetics of the new car were thoroughly analyzed in the press, but no one could comment on performance because no one had driven the car.

BRM team driver Ken Richardson had recently joined Standard-Triumph and was asked to test the 20TS only a few days after the show. Richardson had a long affiliation with Standard during the war years and, after the war, Standard was doing machining work on the BRM V-16 engines.

In an interview with *Triumph Over Triumph* magazine in 1997, Richardson said that he found the car to be an accident on wheels after only a few minutes on the road. Specifically, he noted that the car wallowed, shook, and even jumped sideways. The front suspension flexed under load, steering was imprecise and unpredictable at speed, and the brakes locked easily. "This caused several moments for me that can only be described as very unpleasant adrenaline cocktails," Richardson said. In summary, he went on to describe the prototype as "a complete dog's breakfast."

When writing up his evaluation for Sir John, Richardson thought to himself that it was going to be the end of his job at Standard-Triumph. Instead, Richardson played a key role in polishing the diamond-in-the-rough into a real production sports car. Of course, there was no time to spare because Black demanded the revised car be ready for the Geneva show, a mere four months later.

As feared, the Flying Nine chassis was the root of the prototype's shortcomings. Richardson's team went to work building a new frame. Dimensions from the original form were retained, but an all-new chassis was designed with stronger steel, greater boxing, and relocated cross braces with additional gussets. Richardson road-tested the prototype tirelessly with every change until he was satisfied that it would pass as a production car.

Meanwhile, Belgrove was busy re-styling the 20TS. The front portion of the car was left intact except for relocating the indicator lights into the front apron. The tail of the car was completely redesigned. It was lengthened by 10 inches and given a normal trunk with a proper closing lid. Belgrove came up with the nifty idea of locating the spare wheel in its own compartment below the trunk floor with an access door on the rear panel. He also designed a stylish, removable hardtop using the revolutionary new glass fiber material. However, it was deemed too expensive and tabled until 1954.

Optimism at Standard-Triumph grew with each improvement, but the pressure was on as word of a new MG TF came from Abingdon, and Healey was already in production with the Austin-Healey 100. Then a shot rang out that startled them all. Rootes announced that its new Sunbeam Alpine had broken the 100-mph barrier. The official top speed of 120 mph was achieved by noted rally driver Sheila Van Damm. Focus immediately moved to the Vanguard powerplant;

71 bhp would never do. The edict was power with reliability.

Compression was raised to 8.6:1 from 7:1, which had immediate results of delivering 80 bhp. Intake valve size was increased by 5 percent, valve lift was increased, and camshaft timing was changed for 10 degrees of greater overlap at Top Dead Center. These tweaks yielded an additional 4 bhp. Finally, the twin 1½-inch constant-vacuum down-draft SU carburetors were fitted with new needles that resulted in 90-bhp output.

With each engine upgrade, Richardson dutifully flogged the car on the test track, pushing the engine well past the recommended 5,000 rpm. Cylinder heads cracked, bearings broke, and camshafts bent. Engineers responded to each incident quickly. A redesigned head gasket coupled with extending the head bolts deeper into the block cured the cracking. Lubrication systems were improved to protect the main bearings and a heavier metal in the crankshaft cured the ills.

Power was transmitted through a 9-inch dry clutch to the unchanged Vanguard gearbox. A Laycock de Normanville overdrive was bolted to the rear of the box but was only useable in top gear. The transmission posed no problems during development and was left untouched throughout the process.

After Richardson was regularly and reliably hitting the century mark on the test track, Black ordered him and the TR2 to the Jabbeke Road in Belgium for a speed run. The highway, located in the northwest of Belgium, was something of a Bonneville Salt Flats of Europe where many speed

The prototype 20TS later became the TR1 that launched the iconic TR line of sports cars. The TR1 shown here at the Brussels Auto Show was unveiled at the 1952 Earls Court Motor Show after just eight weeks of gestation. It was created on a very small budget; many of the styling cues seen here were carried over to the final production model. (Photo Courtesy Revs Institute, Karl Ludvigsen Collection)

CHAPTER 2: Triumph's First Sports Car

tests were conducted in the 1950s. What made it so desirable then was that it was a brand-new, smooth concrete highway that was long, straight, and incredibly flat.

On May 20, 1953, a TR2 trimmed with a single diminutive Brooklands-style racing windshield, metal tonneau cover, metal undertray, and rear fender skirts made its first official run. Triumph legend suggests that the seat was removed and Richardson was sitting on a cushion to get as low in the car as possible.

The first two-way run was clocked at just over 104 mph. This was a credible run, but was disheartening to the Triumph crew because everyone felt the potential was much greater. With typical British aplomb, Richardson suggested to the engineers that the car might do better running on all four cylinders rather than three. A plug wire was quickly replaced and on the ensuing run the TR2 topped 124.8 mph, thereby officially launching Triumph's new sports car.

Production of the TR2 began in earnest in July 1953 with just 300 cars produced by year's end. It is ironic that just as Triumph finally established a true production sports car, Sir John Black resigned as managing director. The truth is that Black's underlings were fed up with his management style. They staged something of a coup and forced him out. Black's protégé, Alick Dick, took the reins as Triumph began to hit its stride.

The TR2 compared favorably to MG's new TF model. The Triumph was 151 inches long, 55½ inches wide (383.5 cm), and 50 inches tall (127 cm) with the top up. Coil springs, wishbones, and telescopic shocks were at the front and the live rear axle was fitted with half-elliptic leaf springs. The TF was 147 inches long (373 cm) and just under 60 inches wide (152.4 cm). Its suspension was coil and wishbone up front with half-elliptic leaf springs, similar to the Triumph's, at the rear.

Triumph's 1,991-cc cast-iron wet-sleeved engine produced 90 hp and could propel the car from rest to 60 mph

The 20TS is shown in Coventry on a break from testing by Ken Richardson. The grit and grime of the proving grounds is evident on the side of the car. This view also reveals the sharply curtailed rear end and the exposed spare tire. With the exception of the fender-mounted turn signal indicators, the front section of the car was retained in the final design. (Photo Courtesy British Motor Industry Heritage Trust)

Here, Ken Richardson is all set for his speed test at Jabbeke Road in Belgium in 1953. The TR2 was modified to reduce drag by removing bumpers and including a metal tonneau cover, rear fender skirts, and a belly pan. The full windshield was removed and replaced with a small aero screen. To get as low as possible in the car, Richardson removed the seat and sat on the floor. The TR2 was clocked at 124.889 mph and went into the record books with the highest top speed of the day for a 2-liter production car. (Photo Courtesy British Motor Industry Heritage Trust)

The Jabbeke Road car (serial number MCV575) has recently been restored to its original glory in Wallingford, England. The color of the car is an unusual shade of green. It appears that the car was originally a dark shade of blue, based on the color of the engine compartment. (Photo Courtesy Glen Hewett/Protek Engineering)

The TR2 was the result of Sir John Black's inextinguishable determination to have a popular and financially viable sports car. His primary target was the growing U.S. market after seeing how well MGs were being received across the ocean. The prescript was for a car that was long on performance, short on frills, and that could be built on a tight budget with an even tighter time frame.

The budget-minded grille opening, with its recessed grate, was originally a peculiarity that became a distinctive feature that set the debut model apart from its successors. The initial 20TS prototype had only an opening in the nose, but the recessed mesh grille was added for the production models.

The first of the production "side-screen" Triumphs was the TR2. It was a very smart-looking car considering Black's stipulations that as many common parts as possible be used. In fact, a number of the budget-driven decisions that formed the prototype became iconic features.

CHAPTER 2: Triumph's First Sports Car

The first examples of TR2 production are referred to as "long-door" cars because the full-length doors overlapped inner sills. While cosmetically appealing with no lower sills visible, owners complained about the doors hitting curbs because the cars were already low to the ground.

Midway through the production of the TR2, the doors were redesigned with a shorter length and a visible outer sill, or rocker panel. An additional benefit to the new design was a stronger, stiffer body thanks to reinforced frame rails.

in 11.9 seconds with a top speed of 104 mph. The 1,250-cc MG TF powerplant was rated at 57 hp, reaching 60 mph in 18.9 seconds but was only capable of 80 mph. The clincher was that at £595, the new TR2 was the world's cheapest 100-mph sports car. The TF was priced at £590 and the coveted Jaguar XK120 topped £1,600. The TR2 also delivered a thrifty 30 mpg as well, exceptional for the time.

Early TR2s had an aluminum hood. This can be spotted from outside the car by the rivets in the four corners of the contour in the hood. These cars also used a cable release located under the dashboard on the right-hand side of the car. This was much easier and more convenient than the external Dzus-style fasteners that were adopted for the hood and trunk releases on the balance of the TR2 run and all TR3s. External hinges and fender beading were body color on TR2s. Another identifying feature of early TR2s is that the windshield wipers are closer together on the cowl.

Life inside the TR2 was simple, effective, and functional. Entering the car required reaching in through the side-curtain flap or over the door to a pull-cord. There were neither exterior handles nor locks. The driver sat low in the car and the curved-back bucket seats and cutaway doors combined to give a very open and racy feel.

Ahead of the driver were a large speedometer and tachometer. At the center of the dash was a four-dial cluster featuring fuel, temperature, oil pressure, and ammeter gauges all supplied by Jaeger. Switches for wipers, headlamps, and instrument lights were stacked vertically down the center of the cluster. A manual choke and starter button sat on either side of the ignition lock. A red ignition warning light and amber turn-signal light were also part of the center display. Optional heater and overdrive switches were mounted between the speedometer and outer edge of the cowl. A locking glove box ahead of the passenger with a chrome grab handle just above it added convenience. The diminutive and delicate square rear-view mirror perched atop the cowl.

As production ramped up, Triumph realized that money was to be made by offering a variety of optional add-ons including a heater, overdrive, knock-off wire wheels, rear wheel skirts (also known as spats), Dunlop Road Speed performance tires, and a tool roll. Later options included telescopic steering column, a radio, and the Belgrove fiberglass hardtop.

Road test magazines heaped praise on the new Triumph. The Motor April 1954 issue declared, "We nevertheless rate this as not merely the best sports car available at its price, but also as one of the most promising new models that has been introduced in recent years. Not pared down to minimum weight, especially with a view to use it as a

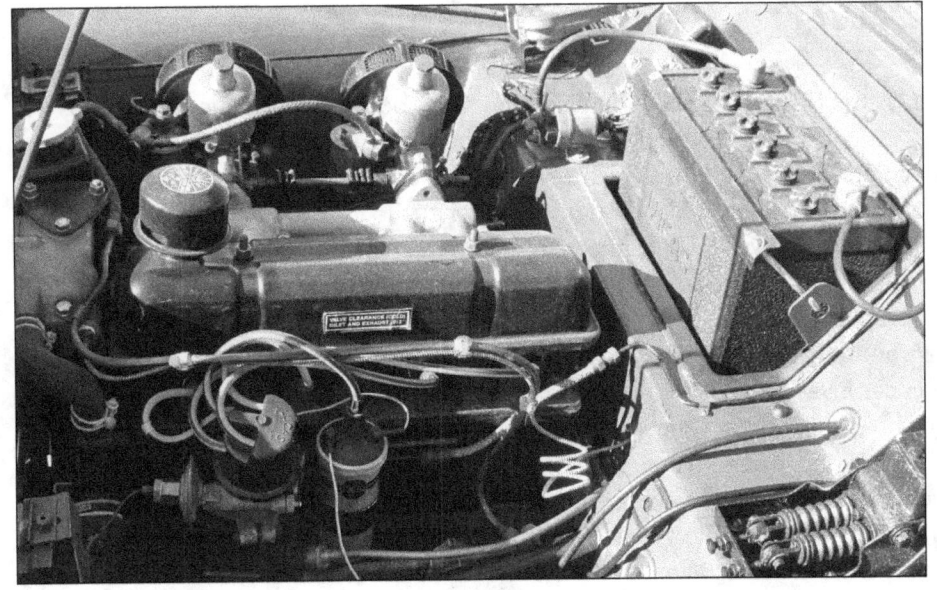

The simple yet rugged 90-hp 1,991-cc Standard Vanguard wet-sleeve engine. Pistons traveled within a sleeve rather than in the block and the sleeves were surrounded by the internal water jacket. The benefits were better cooling and that worn sleeves were easily replaced. Replacing pistons and sleeves could change engine displacement quickly.

competition car, this model offers a combination of comfort, economy, speed, and sheer enjoyment of travel in a responsive open two-seater, which should assure it of very large sales in many parts of the world."

This proved to be true as *Road & Track* raved, "The TR2 will out-drag any stock American car from a standstill."

Racing success at Le Mans, Mille Miglia, Tourist Trophy, and a win at the RAC Rally helped the TR2 catch on all over the world.

Some minor improvements were introduced in the fall of 1954. Most notable was increasing the size of the rear Lockheed hydraulic brakes to a width of 1¾ inches to match the front. The Press had grumbled about brake fade, so this was meant as a fix. The exhaust was made quieter with new mounting points to stop rattles. Springs were softened in reaction to complaints of a harsh ride and the optional electrically actuated overdrive worked in all but first gear. It may sound like a small change, but the availability of essentially three additional gears made the car extremely flexible for in-town driving.

The most obvious cosmetic change to the first-year car was a redesign of the doors. It was actually a redesign of the entire center section of the car. Instead of full-length doors that overlapped the sills, an outer lower sill, or rocker panel, was added to address complaints of hitting tall curbs when exiting the car. The result was a stronger, stiffer body. This is the difference between the "long-door" and "short-door" TR2s.

Early TR2s are also identifiable by the obvious larger "double" thermostat housing at the front of the engine. Only the first 1,200 cars built used this unique design. Later, a conventional single thermostat was adopted and the radiator hoses were relocated.

A starter button was mounted on the firewall on TR2s and TR3s that allowed a mechanic to engage the starter while working under the hood. It was extremely convenient for a solo mechanic, especially while synchronizing the dual SU carburetors.

SWALLOW DORETTI

The name may sound Italian, but the car is strictly British, with a dash of American.

The car was the brainchild of Arthur Andersen and his daughter Dorothy. Andersen was a California-based engineer and inventor. One of his best-known projects was developing the Whizzer engine for use on bicycles. Dorothy was his test driver as he developed the uniquely propelled cycles.

Thanks to her father, Dorothy had an aptitude for all things mechanical. When the British sports car invasion hit California, Dorothy bought an MG T-series. As her father began making accessories for the car, she saw an opportunity and began marketing the luggage racks and other convenience items. Her company was first called Doretti Accessories and later Cal Specialties after the Doretti name was sold to Swallow Coachbuilders for $1.

Cal Specialties operated alongside Cal Sales, which was the Triumph distributor that Andersen headed.

As the business and TR2 sales grew, Arthur was in search of a sports car with all the appointments of an upscale model but with a reasonable price tag similar to a Triumph. Andersen's steel tubing company had connections to the Tube Investments Company in England, which was the parent of Swallow Coach Building. His timing could not have been any better.

In 1952, Tube Investments was looking to separate its industrial side from its coachworks and had a sports car design on the table. Andersen hooked up with designer Eric Saunders; they identified the TR2's body-on-frame running gear as the catalyst for making their dreams come true. On one of his trips to England, Andersen was able to pitch the idea to Sir John Black. Black was never one to turn down money and approved the project. In fact, it resulted in Andersen being appointed the U.S. West-Coast distributor of Standard Triumph.

The design of the car looked like a cross between the TR2 and the Austin-Healey 100 of the same era, but perhaps slightly more like a Nash-Healey. It had far fewer curves than the Triumph and had full-size doors with exterior door handles. The large chrome grille and outboard headlights could have the uneducated mistaking it for a Healey.

Underneath the hand-built aluminum body was a tube frame fitted-out with TR2 suspension and drivetrain. The unique frame provided greater strength and rigidity but the additional length made the car heavier than its donor cousin.

The interior was lavishly trimmed, resulting in a more luxurious appearance than the TR. The contour-less, leather-covered dash used all Triumph instruments but in a very different layout. The tachometer was mounted to the right of the 3-spoke TR2 steering wheel while the speedometer was mounted in front of the passenger next to a grab handle. A central panel, similar to Triumph's, housed four gauges and all necessary switches.

The Swallow Doretti was introduced in 1953 and was sold alongside TR2s in the same showrooms, which made

The Swallow Doretti could be considered a reimagined TR2. Conceived in the United States but built in Britain, the car featured a hand-built aluminum body mounted to an alloy tube frame fitted with TR2 driveline and suspension. It was 3 inches wider than the TR2 and has smoother, more flowing lines as well as such modern conveniences as external door handles. (Photo Courtesy Peter McCann)

The 90-hp 1991-cc Vanguard engine carried straight over into the Doretti. The tubular steel box section chassis allowed the engine to be mounted a few inches back in the car giving it a slightly better weight distribution. The lower hood line necessitated a small bulge to accommodate the dual carburetors; this feature returned a few years later in the TR4. This highly detailed engine compartment features a period-correct optional Doretti valvecover. (Photo Courtesy doretti.com)

The cockpit of the Doretti offered a luxurious take on the TR3 cockpit from which it was derived. Trimmed in leather, the seats were more plush and thanks to the envelope-style body, the full-size doors made for a cozier feeling. The larger cubby compartments in the doors helped make up for the loss of the glove box and it had a small luggage shelf behind the seats. Instrumentation was relocated to the center of the dash, which was not optimal, especially with the tachometer in front of the passenger. This version includes the rare Perspex side curtain with flip-out vent window. (Photo Courtesy doretti.com)

perfect sense when it came to service. The upscale Doretti was priced approximately $400 more than the Triumph. All of the cars were built in Coventry with most of the production earmarked for the United States.

Sir John Black was keenly interested in the project. While on a test drive in an early Doretti with Ken Richardson at the wheel, a truck struck the car outside the Standard Triumph offices. Both men were injured with cuts and some broken bones. The car was a write-off.

Andersen achieved his goal of a stylish yet affordable sports car for its day. Unfortunately, sales were not robust and production ceased in 1955 with just 275 produced. Despite the short-lived Doretti, Cal Sales' role as a major player in Triumph sports car sales in the United States had only just begun. The company was instrumental in selling Triumph cars; it sold more TRs than any other distributor in the country. It had so much clout that it was singled-handedly responsible for the extended production of the first models and the resulting TR3B. On the West Coast, it played a major role in Triumph racing with Kas Kastner's successes on the track.

Dorothy Deen (née Andersen) became a major spokesperson for Triumph and appeared in many advertisements and on television shows. She was also a savvy businesswoman in the man's automotive world of the day. She was one of just two women in all of Triumph's distribution network.

The sad fate of a 1953 Doretti prototype. Test driver Ken Richardson and Sir John Black collided with a truck outside the gates of Triumph's Banner Lane facility. Both occupants were badly injured in the crash. While struggling with his recovery from the wreck, Black was ousted as head of Standard Triumph. (Photo Courtesy British Motor Industry Heritage Trust)

SUCCESS! THE TR3

Just over 8,600 TR2s were produced when the TR3 took its entrance bow in the fall of 1955. Because Standard-Triumph was hard at work on a new Vanguard sedan, only a few changes were introduced that autumn.

The visible differences between the cars were subtle with the obvious exception of the front apron. The old recessed mouth was replaced by a flush-mounted egg-crate grille but still maintained provision for a hand crank. Other cosmetics included stainless steel beading between the

The interior of the TR2 was simple and functional, very much a true sports car. There is ample legroom for both passenger and driver with legs outstretched alongside the transmission tunnel. Wind noise and buffeting is surprisingly scant considering how open the car appears.

It would not be a sports car without the fashionable full complement of instruments telling the driver everything he or she needed to know. A large speedometer and tachometer were mounted directly ahead of the driver with supplemental engine monitoring in the center section of the dashboard. Overdrive was not available on early cars.

The spare tire was housed on its own compartment below the trunk. Access was through the lower panel at the back of the car. Early TR2s are also identified by the smaller, square taillights. Only the center lamp lit when the brake was applied. The corner lights served only as turn signals, also known as trafficators.

Seats were relatively comfortable for the time with overly sprung seat bottoms and slightly curved seatbacks for moderate support. Creature comforts such as a heater was an optional add-on. Seatbelts were not originally offered but were frequently purchased as an aftermarket item.

This 1956 TR3 illustrates the most significant design difference from the TR2. The egg-crate grille was brought forward to be flush with the front apron and trimmed to look more finished. A subsequent redesign of the apron for the TR3A explains why these cars are referred to as "small-mouth" 3s.

The tonneau cover could be snapped into place easily to either completely cover the cockpit or leave the driver's side open. This feature allowed for open-air motoring but eliminated the drafts entering from the passenger's side on a cool day.

The arrival of the new TR3 was much heralded by the motor press. *Road & Track* splashed the new car on the cover of the June 1956 issue. The car appeared with the optional factory hardtop. (Photo Courtesy *Road & Track*)

This version is spec'd with 48-spoke wire wheels and four-wheel drum brakes. Budget-minded buyers could specify steel wheels with hubcaps. The 11-inch Girling front disc brakes were introduced on the 1956 TR3, making it the first production car to offer disc brakes.

CHAPTER 2: Triumph's First Sports Car

For the TR3, the 1,991 Standard Vanguard engine was rated at 95 hp through the aid of bigger 1¾-inch SU carburetors. The unique design of the wet-sleeve engine with its pistons operating inside removable cylinders made for easier maintenance and performance upgrades. Theoretically, worn sleeves could be changed easily and engine displacement could be modified with new sleeves and pistons.

fenders and body as well as chrome hinges. Both were previously body-colored. The tool roll, previously optional, became standard equipment.

Interior door panels were re-contoured to provide additional width for driver and passenger. The seats were located slightly forward to make room for the optional rear "seat," which was actually little more than an upholstered parcel shelf. An adult would not have any legroom so it was really only suitable for a small child. The safety standards of the day were definitely not the same as today.

The important changes were far less visible. Horsepower output was boosted to 95 by ditching the original 1½-inch SU carbs in favor of the larger barreled 1¾-inch units. Overdrive was added to second and third gear to afford a seven-speed range. In mid-1956, the high-port head with semi-spherical combustion chambers, proven in the factory Le Mans effort, was adopted. These successive upgrades allowed Triumph to officially boast a true 100-hp sports car. This delivered a new top speed of 110 mph. However, the 0-60–mph times dropped by .4. No official torque figures

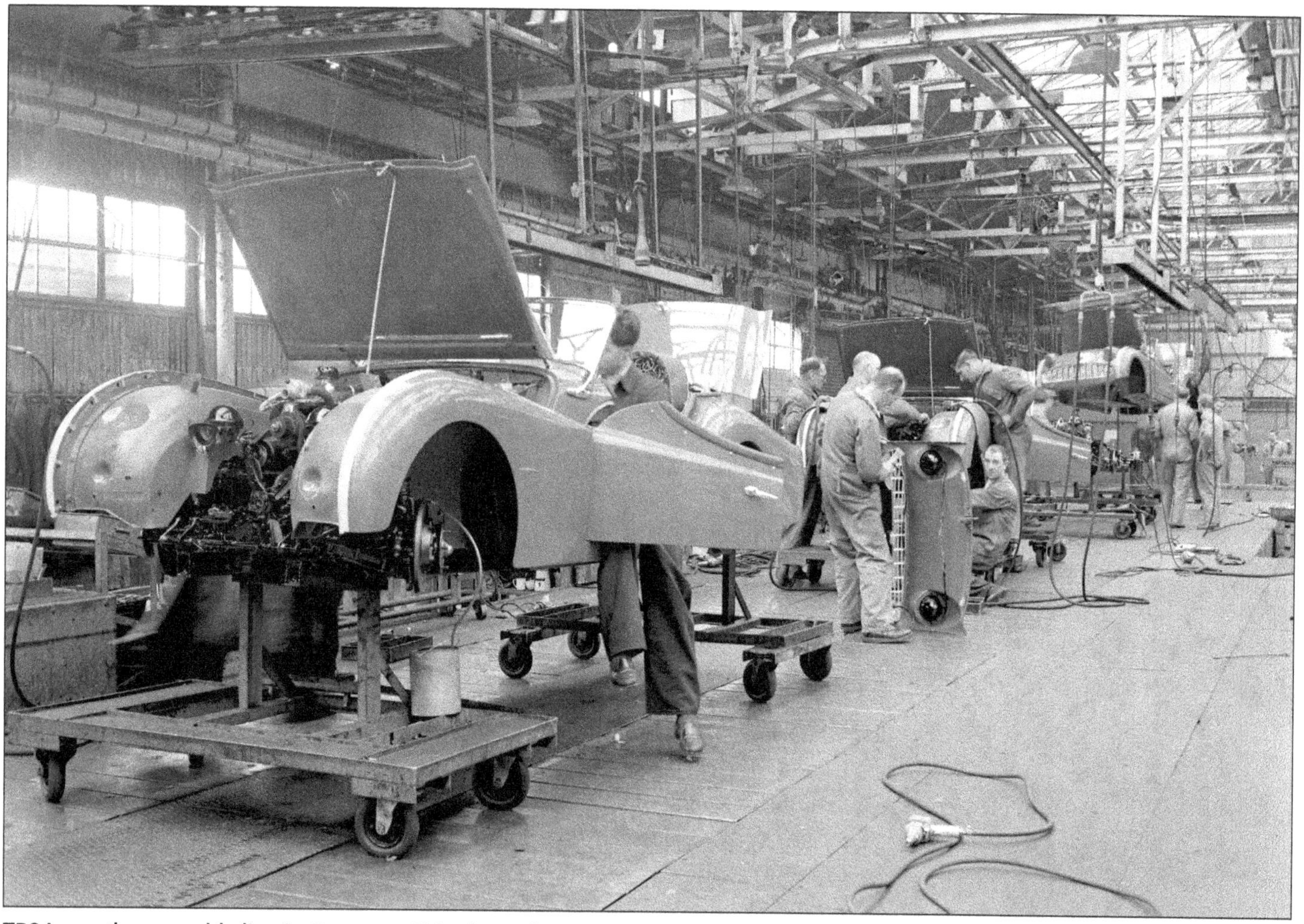

TR3As on the assembly line in Coventry. This photo illustrates how the cars were very much bolted together from the inside out. The car in the foreground is having the Girling disc brakes bled. (Photo Courtesy British Motor Industry Heritage Trust)

were released for the TR3; however, the TR2 boasted 117 ft-lbs, so you could assume that the figure rests somewhere between the TR2 and the 127 ft-lbs in the forthcoming TR4.

The Triumph was still a fast car and a fine value at £680. *Car Life* said, "For a man who wants to get a lot of basic sports car for a low price, the TR3 is hard to beat." The more refined, new MGA, introduced a year earlier sold for £610 with a 1,500-cc engine rated at a paltry 68 hp.

The 1957 TR3 made history when it featured Girling 11-inch front disc brakes as standard equipment. Of course, Triumph was not the first disc-brake car; Jaguar's C-Type sports/racer and Colin Chapman's Lotus Eleven had run with four-wheel discs and Chrysler, Crosley, and Citroën had offered them at various points in the early 1950s. However, Triumph was the first mass-production car to offer the new stopping technology as standard equipment.

Why not discs at all four wheels? Triumph found that the disc/drum combination was successful, or at least more than adequate for the car. Most important, the setup was less expensive. Moreover, at the time, rear discs were unreliable as parking brakes.

At the same time, the old Mayflower rear axle was replaced by a more stout assembly taken from the Vanguard III production.

Factory options on the car included heater, race screens, wire wheels with center knock-offs, leather upholstery, fiberglass hardtop, telescoping steering column, overdrive, a chrome passenger grab handle, and rear fender skirts.

Sales were soaring, but the TR3 was to last for only two model years with slightly more than 13,000 units produced. The follow-up TR3A model carried the torch for four model years and more than 58,000 units.

TR3 Becomes an International Success

More than 13,300 TR3s had been minted when the TR3A was introduced. The TR3A was virtually unchanged from the previous "3" when it arrived in 1958. The engine and running gear remained identical to the previous car, but it received a number of cosmetic changes. A full-width, stamped aluminum grille was added and modern conveniences such as door handles and a trunk lid handle were now standard. The headlight pods on the front apron were recessed slightly and, for the first time, the name "Triumph"

The rear of the TR3A took another step toward visibility and safety. Additional brake lamps were added along with a chrome housing for the license plate light. The Dzus fasteners on the trunk lid were deleted in favor of the locking handle. The TR3A was the first model to include the manufacturer's name in chrome letters.

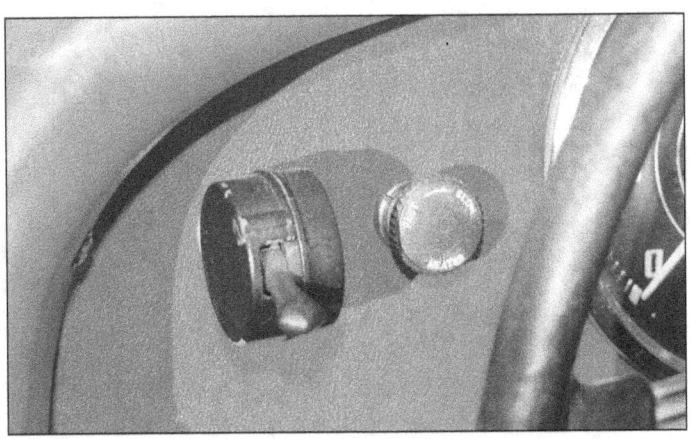

Gauges and switches remained the same; however, an electrically operated overdrive was added as an option. The Laycock de Normanville unit was available in second, third, and fourth gears, making the car more versatile for both city and highway driving. The control knob for the optional heater is visible at the right.

The interior was largely unchanged for the TR3. The Smiths instruments were laid out similarly to its predecessor. A pull knob was added at the top center of the dashboard to open a small flap just ahead of the windshield. When opened, fresh air was channeled directly to the footwells to help dissipate engine heat.

CHAPTER 2: Triumph's First Sports Car

The rear turn-signal lenses were enlarged and rounded. From the TR3 onward, the external hinges and fender beading were chrome.

The TR3A debuted in 1958 and quickly became the best-selling of all the side-screen cars. The wider stamped aluminum grille was the most obvious change to the car.

The running gear in the 3A remained the same as its predecessor. In 1959, the engine was re-sleeved up to 2,138 cc. The larger displacement, coupled with a higher-compression head, delivered a true 100 hp.

With the 3A, the Triumph name appeared on the car for the first time. Individual chrome letters were fastened across the front apron and the hood badge was changed from red and black to blue and white.

appeared on the front and rear of the car, spelled out in individual chrome letters.

Under the hood, the burly Vanguard engine continued to do yeoman's duty, churning out a reliable 100 hp. By this time, the high-port head with the semi-spherical combustion chambers was a standard production item, despite its slightly haphazard introduction. Torque was measured at 117 ft-lbs and the 0-60–mph time remained a tick over 12 seconds.

With more than 58,000 cars sold by 1961, the TR3A proved to be the most popular and most prolific of all Triumphs to date. That was more than four times the TR3 figure and nearly twice the next-best-selling Triumph, the 1950–1953 Mayflower Saloon.

Late in the TR3A production run, the trusty 1,991-cc mill was re-sleeved to produce an optional 2,138-cc engine. The larger sleeves increased bore by 3 mm to 86 mm and compression was raised from 8.5:1 to 9.1:1. These engines were optional in 1959 and adopted in 1960. In 1962, a U.S.-only TR3B was offered. While the car was advertised as a B, it was not officially badged as such. It was

The interior also remained unchanged in the 3A with the same gauge layout. In an effort to add comfort, additional padding was put into the seats. Unfortunately the result was formless, featureless seats with little support. Comfort remained relative.

identical to its predecessor except that it was fitted with the 2,138-cc engine.

This new B model helped Triumph keep the car alive in the United States and stall for time because the TR3's successor was delayed. The B also helped deplete the parts inventory. The entire manufacturing run of 3,331 TR3Bs were sent to the United States.

In eight short years Triumph had established itself as a prominent sports car manufacturer offering reliable, robust performance at a fair price. But time was running out on the 3 design and sales were slowing, especially in the British market.

Sports car buyers were becoming less tolerant of the bare-bones nature and rugged ride of the Triumph. Cars such as the MGA and Sunbeam Alpine offered more options and more comfort with similar performance and a competitive price. Triumph needed to react quickly.

As the TR4 was being unveiled, there was still a significant number of TR3A parts in inventory. This beefier version is actually on a slightly wider TR4 chassis. A small number of TR3Bs were offered alongside the new model. An evolution of the grille differentiated the cars. The concept also featured enlarged stone guards on the rear fenders. Ultimately, 3Bs were simply 3As with a different designation. (Photo Courtesy British Motor Industry Heritage Trust)

The TR2, TR3, and TR3A represented the epitome of open-air sports cars of the 1950s. Built on a shoestring budget and rushed to market in mere months, the cars delivered on the original mandate of performance and value. With more than 83,000 copies sold, side-screen Triumphs defined a generation of British sports cars. (Photo Courtesy David Gooley)

Triumph also introduced external door handles and an external trunk handle for the new model, which are the most telling features of the new model. The Dzus-style spring-loaded hood pins carried over from the previous cars but were deleted on the trunk.

CHAPTER 3

THE ITALIAN JOB

Giovanni Michelotti (left) with managing director Alick Dick (right) stand alongside a newly minted Herald on display. Michelotti was an Italian automobile stylist based in Turin who worked with Ferrari and Maserati throughout his career. He was responsible for many of Triumph's significant designs of the 1960s. Michelotti's first official design for Triumph was the Herald when he rescued a styling disaster at the last minute and created a stylish small car that became a timely sales success. (Photo Courtesy British Motor Industry Heritage Trust)

Thoughts of a TR3 successor actually began as early as 1956, just as the TR3 was beginning to take off, but Triumph was again struggling, both financially and stylistically. At this point, the TR hadn't completely taken off and the cost of re-tooling the factory for a new design was out of the question.

Sedan sales were declining. The stumpy, lumpy 8 and 10 Standard sedans were also in desperate need of a makeover; both cars had a direct ancestry to early pre-war cars originally named for their respective horsepower outputs. They were reinvented twice as the Flying 8 and 10 just before World War II and finally as Standards in the 1950s. The only real cash flow at Standard-Triumph, apart from the TRs, was generated by the manufacture of engines for Ferguson tractors.

The Standard 8 was offered from 1953 to 1959. It is the descendent of the Flying 8 introduced in 1938 and named for its 8-hp output. After the war, the economical four-door was reintroduced as the Standard with a 26-hp 803-cc engine. This Gold Star version featured the 30-hp engine and nicer interior trim. (Photo Courtesy Simon Goldsworthy/*Triumph World*)

In 1954, Triumph introduced the Standard 10, which was based on the same platform as the 8 but with finer appointments, a 948-cc 33-hp engine, and an optional semi-automatic gearbox. The ancestry of the 10 is similar to the 8; the original 10-hp was introduced in 1914 and evolved through the Flying 10 until production ceased during the war. This estate version was known as the Companion. (Photo Courtesy Simon Goldsworthy/*Triumph World*)

The Standard Pennant of 1957 marked the last evolution of the 8/10 platform. Pennant power was increased to 37 bhp and it came with a host of luxury options including a heater, radio, and leather seats. Pennants received status items such as two-tone paint and a mild fin treatment on the rear fenders. A small number were exported to the United States and sold as TR-10s. (Photo Courtesy Simon Goldsworthy/*Triumph World*)

CHAPTER 3: The Italian Job

The 1957 TR Dream Car (right) came about through a chance meeting between Alick Dick and Michelotti. The Dream Car was based on the TR3 chassis and was only meant to be a show car, not a production car. The styling elements including the rear fins and inset body accent flash were popular at this time. It's impossible not to see some of the styling elements that became part of the new TR4. The Zoom prototype (left) came about later in TR4 development. (Photo Courtesy British Motor Industry Heritage Trust)

Alick Dick was in a tough spot. He needed a new sedan, a replacement for an aging sports car, and the cash to accomplish it all. Or perhaps even a buyer for the entire company. Instead, he was able to sell the tractor-making operation to Massey-Harris of Canada. This generated several million pounds of much needed capital to solve his styling and production woes. It has been noticed that the tractor sale coincided with the point when the TR badge changed from black and red to blue and white.

In 1957, Triumph hired Giovanni Michelotti from Turin, Italy, as a consultant-designer to help with the new sedans and to take on the TR3 replacement. Michelotti was an up-and-coming designer who had recently left Vignale Carrozzeria to strike out on his own.

After a chance meeting with Dick at a motor show, he was asked to design a TR Dream Car based on the TR3 frame; it was an audition of sorts. His timing was fortuitous because as Michelotti was delivering his concepts, the Triumph team was in dire straits with its new sedan.

Styling for the new Herald was a mess. Walter Belgrove had left the company abruptly following a disagreement over the direction of the car. Everyone knew that the car they had come up with was not going to be well received by the public.

There was also a paranoia of sorts regarding the competition, particularly Austin, which was now part of BMC and had plenty of cash for development. The new car was being developed under the code name SC for small car. Obviously anyone could figure this out so Harry Webster had a list of names made beginning with the letter Z. With no rhyme or reason to the names, no one could tell what kind of car was in development. The SC became project Zobo. I have no idea what the level of industrial espionage was at this time, but if SC was a dead giveaway for small car, it is assured that no one could divine what Zobo meant.

MICHELOTTI TO THE RESCUE

Michelotti rescued Triumph's sedan in the 11th hour. He tossed out the Triumph designers' work and redesigned the entire body. His prototype, built in Italy, arrived in Covington late in 1957, and the unique body-on-frame layout bowled over Triumph management.

It was love at first sight as Triumph's management received the best Christmas present it could have ever

Michelotti's first concept to replace the TR3 was known as code name Zest. At this time, Triumph was concerned about competition from the other British carmakers so it came up with meaningless words for projects in development so no one could tell what they were working on. This design is obviously very close to the final TR4 design. (Photo Courtesy British Motor Industry Heritage Trust)

The original Herald coupe was the first official project designed by Giovanni Michelotti. As legend has it, after a great deal of internal strife over the design of the successor to the Standard 8 and 10, Michelotti was called in. He sketched a design in a matter of minutes that became the Herald. The body-on-chassis design was an immediate hit and featured the unique forward-tilting front clip that provided incredible access to the 948-cc engine and front suspension. The chassis and distinct hood design carried over to the Spitfire. (Photo Courtesy Simon Goldsworthy/*Triumph World*)

Born out of the never-ending quest for more power and performance, the Vitesse debuted in 1962. Also known as the Sports Six in the United States, the original car offered the 1,596-cc inline 6-cylinder engine mated with a 4-speed manual gearbox and optional overdrive. The forward-pivoting front bodywork was redesigned by Michelotti to accommodate the larger power unit. In 1966, the Vitesse received the 1,998-cc engine and was marketed as the 2-liter. (Photo Courtesy Simon Goldsworthy/*Triumph World*)

hoped for. The new car was named the Herald after Alick Dick's boat and it became a quick and much-needed success. The unique rear swing axle gave the car four-wheel independent suspension. The hood and fenders were all one piece and pivoted forward for amazing access to the engine. The 25-foot turning radius was simply incredible. These attributes also turned out to be the genesis for a special project five years later.

As project Zobo came to fruition in the form of the Herald, Michelotti's real work began on project Zest, the successor to the TR3. The charter for the new car included more creature comforts in the cabin, including more space and wind-up windows. The body design also needed to be much more contemporary.

Many of these concepts were already incorporated into Michelotti's TR3 Dream Car. The show car, built by Vignale, was bold and aggressive for its time with black and white two-tone bodywork and dripping with contemporary American influences including a full-width gaping chrome grille, and pronounced tail fins that were exaggerated by the two-tone paint. The interior was lavishly appointed and included the much-debated wind-up windows.

Although it was strictly a styling exercise mounted on an unmodified TR3 chassis, several styling cues influenced future Triumphs. One such element was the full-width grille that inspired the front-end revision on the TR3A.

After its brief show tour, the Dream Car was brought to Coventry for the Triumph team to absorb and ponder its various attributes. They liked many things, but it was determined that it would be too expensive to tool-up to build it. They were also concerned that the overt styling cues would become dated rapidly.

Michelotti's first Zest prototype was completed and delivered to Triumph in early 1958 for evaluation. Because of the many similarities, this first rendition is best described as the ultra-conservative brother of the Dream Car. Zest still

The Zoom prototype was a variation on the Zest concept but with an eye toward incorporating the larger twin-cam Sabrina engine. The Zoom had a 4-inch-wider track and 6-inch-longer wheelbase. The project was scrapped when it was determined that the engine was not viable for production. (Photo Courtesy British Motor Industry Heritage Trust)

CHAPTER 3: The Italian Job

Shortly after World War II came to a close, and Sir John Black was trying to build a sports car modeled after the SS100, Jaguar unveiled the XK120 prototype at the London Motor Show. Public reception to the open two-seater was so great that William Lyons put the car into production with the first models completed in 1948. Passengers were swaddled in leather and, despite having abbreviated doors and side curtains, they were actually well protected from the elements. Eventually, a drophead coupe was offered with a padded top that folded down behind the seats. It was easier to operate, but it didn't tuck completely out of sight and sat bunched up on the rear deck. (Photo Courtesy Classic Car Garage)

had a flat nose with a full-width, less ostentatious chrome grille and a modest tail fin at the squared-off rear end. The headlamps had been moved from the top of the fenders into the grille but retained the eyebrows that became contours at the leading edge of the hood. The semi-wraparound windshield was identical to that of the show car.

The dashboard, steering wheel, and external chrome hinges were brought over from the TR3A. Even the tuck-under spare tire compartment was centered between the split rear bumpers.

An unmodified TR3A frame was used, but it was beginning to fall from favor because the press had dubbed it too narrow for sure-footed handling. It was also not particularly complementary to this new design, which begged for a wider stance to provide for a roomier cockpit and the thicker doors. The goal was to have the new Zest/TR4 on the market by 1959. Unfortunately, the new Herald gobbled up the resources and the debut was delayed.

While management took turns driving and evaluating Zest, the Competitions department was hard at work on a new racing powerplant targeted for the 24-hour race at Le Mans. The fruits of their labor was a 2-liter twin-cam 4-cylinder making nearly 160 hp. The engine was officially known as 20X, but later nicknamed Sabrina after a well-known buxom British movie starlet because of the pronounced, round twin-cam covers.

Sabrina was placed in a modified TR3A to race at Le Mans in 1959. The TR3 "S" had a heavier frame, 6-inch-longer wheelbase, and Perspex acrylic windshield that wrapped around the sides of the cockpit. Although the cars did not finish, Sabrina showed great promise. Alick Dick was so excited by the potential of the engine that he wanted to offer a street version as an option and asked Michelotti to design a car around it.

Unfortunately, Sabrina's unique design was neither trim nor petite and required a completely different frame to carry its girth. This new project car, code named Zoom, was delivered a short time later looking rather like Zest with a 6-inch-longer wheelbase and 4-inch-wider track. Apart from the obvious extra sheet metal between the front wheel and door, the Zoom received a new nose, no eyebrows, a stylish grille, and a complementary convertible top. This top treatment was much better than the attempt to fit the quirky-looking Herald hardtop in the first exercise.

Under the hood was a DOHC inline 3.4-liter 6-cylinder pumping out 160 hp capable of 125 mph. Fed by twin SU carburetors, it could go from rest to 60 mph in 10 seconds. Subsequent models, the XK140 and XK150, were styled similarly and featured increased engine displacement and horsepower; they peaked in 1960 with 3.8 liters and 265 hp. (Photo Courtesy Classic Car Garage)

The B Series engine featured a cast-iron block and head with three main bearings. Fuel was delivered via twin SU carbs. This engine was initially designed at 1.2 liters but was expanded to 1.5 liters, and eventually 1.8 liters with five main bearings. These rugged 4-cylinders were BMC's most heavily used engine; it was installed in at least seven car models and at least one tractor between 1954 and 1980. (Photo Courtesy Classic Car Garage)

Michelotti had also proposed an interesting two-piece steel hardtop with a detachable center section for the new car.

Triumph management picked the Zoom almost instantly as the leading contender to succeed the TR3, but in the end it was determined that a de-tuned Sabrina engine would be too costly to put into production. It is again unfortunate that Triumph missed an opportunity to offer a twin-cam performance engine. Jaguar had been building a market share steadily with its DOHC 6-cylinder and even MG had a brief foray with the MGA 1600 Twincam in 1958. Nevertheless, Dick and company saw the benefit of having the new sports car tied to the company's racing campaign and the TR4 project was finally put into high gear.

I say *finally* because anyone looking at this process from the outside, whether or not they were in the automotive industry, would acknowledge that the gestation period for the new model was far too long. Even Michelotti moved more quickly than Triumph when he partnered with Vignale Carrozzeria of Turin to build the Triumph Italia. The very stylish coupe was one of Michelotti's prototype designs that debuted in 1958. The two-seater hardtop sat on unmodified TR3A and TR3B chassis using the 1,991-cc engines. Chassis were sold and shipped to Turin as needed, which is why the car spanned TR3A and 3B serial numbers. Production is said to have been extremely limited but no actual figures exist. The Italia was available from 1959 through 1962.

Historians have always pegged MG as Triumph's chief competitor throughout the 1950s and 1960s. This is logical given the two marques' style, layout, performance, and price. The MGA arrived in the fall of 1955 as the successor to the aging T-series. The modern envelope body was mounted on an evolution of the T-series frame. Power came from an inline 1,489-cc 4-cylinder making 68 hp through twin SU carburetors. MGA production lasted seven years with slightly more than 101,000 units produced. (Photo Courtesy Classic Car Garage)

CHAPTER 3: The Italian Job

ITALIA 2000 GT

The Italia was easily the most enigmatic of all the Triumphs ever built and despite its name, country of origin, and manufacturer, the car was a Triumph through and through.

While Michelotti was hard at work on the TR3's successor and Herald sedan, Vignale built the car with the hope of getting Triumph to choose its design. The Italia 2000 GT, as it is formally known, made its debut at the Turin Auto Show in 1958. It was quite obviously a blend of the Zest and Zoom prototypes and shared many styling queues with the eventual TR4. It had an aluminum body fitted to a modified TR3-type frame and running gear but was said to be able to accommodate the Sabrina engine.

A 4-cylinder car was delivered to Coventry in 1958 for evaluation, but

From every angle, the coupe looked like an Italian GT car that would be right at home among the thoroughbred cars of the era. Some suggest that the grille bears a resemblance to the Ferrari 250 SWB. (Photo Courtesy Karl Stokes)

With permission from Triumph, Michelotti created his own version of the new car, called the Italia 2000 GT. The body was built by Vignale and elements of both the Zest and Zoom prototypes could be seen in the final product. Over time it became referred to as simply Italia. (Photo Courtesy Karl Stokes)

Body panels on the original 1958 concept were created from hand-formed aluminum. Part of the goal of creating the full-size mock-up was to convince Triumph to move ahead with this design as the successor to the TR3. It was delivered to Coventry for evaluation, but nothing came of it. Triumph gave Michelotti permission to create and sell his own versions. The car made its first appearance at the 1959 Turin Motor Show. Slightly more than 300 cars were built. (Photo Courtesy Karl Stokes)

Although the car exuded Italian style on the outside, it was all TR3 under the skin. The body was fitted to a production TR3 frame and powered by the same 2-liter wet-sleeve mill. Because Triumph was hoping to have the Sabrina engine available for mass production, the engine bay of the Italia was designed large enough to house the twin-cam. Alas, that did not come to be. (Photo Courtesy Karl Stokes)

Inside and out, this was a luxury GT car fitting for the times. Triumph gauges and switches were used in the Italia. However, when the car was redesigned in this style there was no indication that this car was based in Britain. The manufacturer's suggested retail price (MSRP) was $5,000, nearly double the sticker price of a TR3A and equal to the E-Type Jaguar. It was a difficult selling proposition with no dealer network and no spare body parts. (Photo Courtesy Karl Stokes)

ITALIA 2000 GT CONTINUED

the factory did little with it. Ruffino S.p.A., the Italian Triumph importer, obtained permission to put the car into production. The car was restyled mildly with a steel body as well as a TR3A engine and chassis for its 1959 appearance at the Turin Show.

The Italia did resemble the TR4 in many ways but had a more graceful, feminine line to it. The nose was quite like the Ferrari 250GT while the roof lines might have been likened to an Alfa-Romeo GTA. Inside the GT cabin, it was strictly a two-seater with a stylish and very Italian dash layout.

The car was going to be marketed through Triumph dealers at $5,000, which was a tall order when the same money would buy a Jaguar E-Type. Hindering sales even further was the fact that buyers had to sign a contract that included, among other things, a clause stating that there were no spare body panels in the event of an accident.

Just as the car was about to go into production in mid-1959, Triumph got cold feet because it did not want this new car to compete with the forthcoming TR4. Approximately 300 cars were built and many languished on lots for several years before being sold.

The Italia 2000 GT showcased some of Michelotti's best work to date. Had this design and the 160-hp twin-cam engine become the new car that Alick Dick was searching for, it could have substantially re-charted the fortunes of Triumph. (Photo Courtesy Karl Stokes)

ZOOMING TO THE MARKET

With the Italia being offered in Italy and with the demise of the production twin-cam engine, Michelotti was hard at work marrying the Zest and Zoom concepts into the TR4. The final version was radically different from the established shape and character that had founded Triumph's sporting image. However, high marks and praise were given when the public met the TR4 for the first time in August 1961. Michelotti's styling was well-received and the new creature comforts, including roll-up windows, cockpit ventilation, and an all-synchromesh gearbox, were instantly applauded.

Originally, the windshield was meant to be detachable, at least in concept, and the front and rear fenders were bolted on as with the previous TRs. However, Michelotti's use of a full-width hood, grille, and trunk lid beautifully disguised the crudeness of the manufacturing methods. The rear fender tops and taillight extensions took a cue from the tail-fin phenomenon in America. However, they were much understated, which gave the car a contemporary appeal without the risk of becoming dated. They were certainly less pronounced than the Sunbeam Alpine fins introduced two years earlier.

The DOHC 2-liter Le Mans engine used in competition from 1959 to 1961 was fed by dual twin-choke SU carburetors and rated at 160 hp. It was hoped that it would be the engine of the future, but it proved to be too difficult to produce and too heavy for the street cars. It was nicknamed Sabrina because the bulbous cam covers were likened to a contemporary movie starlet. (Photo Courtesy Revs Institute/George Phillips Collection)

The TRS Le Mans car that was taken from the Zoom concept. The wheelbase was lengthened by 6 inches from the donor TR3A chassis to help accommodate the 150-hp Sabrina twin-cam engine. Three versions of the TRs were entered into the 1960 and 1961 24 Hours of Le Mans. They all failed to finish in 1960 but the following year finished 9th, 11th, and 15th. (Photo Courtesy James Pitt)

Michelotti's Zest concept gave way to the TR4 in 1961 and marked a huge leap forward for Triumph. The fixed curved windshield, full-sized doors, and roomier cockpit acknowledged that the sports car audience was looking for more comfort and protection from the elements. It is shown here with standard steel wheels and hubcaps. Wire wheels were still quite fashionable but were an option. (Photo Courtesy John Myers)

Harry Webster was Triumph's head of engineering from 1957 to 1968. He had actually joined Standard prior to World War II, but began working at Triumph when it was acquired in 1946. Webster was responsible for many of Triumph's designs. He went on to become Technical Director for British Leyland after the merger, succeeding Alec Issigonis, creator of the Mini. (Photo Courtesy British Motor Industry Heritage Trust)

Michelotti's genius is evidenced in the TR4 with a bold new sports car that matched the times. The beautiful lines disguised the rudimentary manufacturing techniques. The slight overhang at the front of the hood was straight from the Zest concept. The teardrop-shaped bubble on the right-hand side was incorporated to clear the carburetors while maintaining the lower hood line.

The hood was distinct because of the forward overhang that created visors above the headlights and the off-center, oblong bulge that was necessary to clear the dual SU HS6 carburetors. The hood also pivoted forward and vertically for better engine access.

A locking trunk was still standard and cargo capacity was increased with the new squared-off design. However, the full-size spare tire no longer had its own cubby but shared space with the luggage beneath the trunk floor.

Although the outer skins and redesigned cockpit were seen as new, the car was still a TR3 at heart. The wheelbase was the same at 7 feet 4 inches, but the front track was increased by 4 inches to 4 feet 1 inch and the rear track increased by 2½ inches to 4 feet. Not only did the wider stance give the car better road-holding ability, it also allowed for a roomier cockpit with 3 more inches of overall width.

The TR3 coil-over-shock front suspension and live rear axle were also used along with the 11-inch front disc brakes and 9-inch rear drums. Rack-and-pinion steering replaced the old cam-and-lever setup. A telescoping steering column was also available.

The first TR4 arrived in August 1961 to critical acclaim. The more contemporary styling, full-envelope body, and creature comforts in the cockpit made it the perfect Triumph for the times. Styling elements from Michelotti's prototypes can be seen in the nose and tail. Steel wheels and "dog dish" center caps were standard equipment. The 48-spoke wire wheels were optional.

To give the car the appearance of a wider track, especially because it was essentially still a TR3 underneath, the stamped aluminum grille ran the full width of the car. Hinges were moved under the skin and the full-length hood tipped forward. The slot for the hand crank was still retained. Hand cranking this engine was very difficult and not terribly effective.

This allowed the driver more space as needed and it also served as a safety item because it collapsed on impact.

The bigger, better, new TR tipped the scales at 2,128 pounds, nearly 80 pounds heavier than its predecessor. Helping to compensate for the extra mass was the re-sleeved Vanguard 4-cylinder with a 3-mm larger bore, which brought displacement to 2,138 cc. Outwardly, the engine looked identical to the earlier version but delivered 105 hp at 4,600 rpm and boosted torque to 127 ft-lbs at 3,350 rpm. The first TR4 posted a 0-60–mph time of 10.9 seconds and the quarter-mile was covered in 17.8 seconds, nipping the TR3 on both counts. However, top speed remained unchanged at 102 mph.

As with the underpinnings, many of the soft parts also came from TR3 stock. Seats, instruments, and steering wheel were a direct carryover. Despite the updated fascia, the layout was similar to the TR3 with larger speedo and tach in front of the driver and the balance of the gauges and switches in a center cluster. A locking glove box remained standard and Triumph's through-dash ventilation was a first. Previously, all vents pointed to the footwells. Options included wire wheels, luggage rack, radio, heater, sun visors, windshield washer, and a rear seat/parcel shelf. The Laycock de Normanville overdrive was also available in three forward speeds. Engaging the overdrive was moved from a toggle on the dashboard to a stalk on the steering column diametrically opposed to the turn indicator lever.

The optional Michelotti-designed hardtop featured the nifty removable center roof panel. When the top piece was removed, the aft section provided excellent wind protection

By the time the TR4 came to market, the craze for big fins had pretty much passed. However, styling in the early 1960s still incorporated fin-like flair on the rear flanks. The hint of rear fins is unmistakable at the rear of Michelotti's new design. Rather than having its own separate compartment, as it did on the TR3, the spare tire was moved inside the more-spacious trunk.

but still gave the feel of open-car motoring, especially with the large wraparound rear glass. Unfortunately, there was no provision for carrying the removable panel in the car so a section of folding convertible top was offered. The design was dubbed the Surrey top, but the name never quite stuck to anything but the TR4.

Years later car builders such as Porsche and Fiat had the world referring to the same design as a Targa top. Once again, Triumph design was ahead of its time, but the concept slipped through its fingers when it did not gain traction in the market. The Surrey-topped cars never really caught on until the 1990s when the cars became collectible and the unique top was seen as a valuable option.

Despite the goals to tie the road cars to the competition models, shortly after the TR4 was unveiled the TRS competition program was shut down and there were no marketing ties between the two cars.

Triumph's unique Surrey top featured the equivalent of the rear portion of a hardtop complete with a glass rear window. A removable canvas panel bridged the gap between the windshield header and the aft section. The rear section was held in place with bolts similar to a removable hardtop. (Photo Courtesy Classic Car Garage)

The precursor to the Targa top was stylish and reduced wind drafts at speed. Later in the production run, a metal center section was available that made the car even more airtight. (Photo Courtesy Classic Car Garage)

The cut doors of the TR3 line that harkened back to pre-war styling were finally gone. The new body of the TR4 featured full-sized doors with roll-up windows. The complement of instruments carried over from its predecessor, but they were nicely incorporated into the wood-veneer fascia. (Photo Courtesy Classic Car Garage)

The TR4 was a handsome car from every angle. The rear view is one of the most distinctive because it all worked. This is more true in retrospect because its successor, 10 years later, was starkly different. The integration of "cathedral"-style taillamps helped make the design work. The lenses were remarkably similar to the contemporary Aston Martin DB4 and it has been suggested that they are interchangeable between the two marques. This is unlikely.

The October 1961 edition of *Road & Track* featured the new TR4 on the cover. Its first impressions of the car were positive and it called the car "modern and homogenous." *Car and Driver* called it "the best-looking and most comfortable sport Triumph made." (Photos Courtesy *Road & Track/Car and Driver*)

The Jaguar XK-E burst onto the automotive scene in 1961 with the perfect combination of performance and beauty. The car was like nothing that had come out of Britain before. The DOHC 3.8-liter inline-6 was fed by a triple set of SU carburetors making 265 hp and a top speed of 150 mph. The E-Type's standard equipment was also unrivaled with independent suspension, disc brakes, and rack-and-pinion steering. (Photo Courtesy Classic Car Garage)

Although motoring journalists had good things to say about the TR4, it was obvious that they were a bit disappointed in the lack of development in some areas. *Road & Track* said, "The TR4 offers excellent performance at a moderate initial cost and a sporting driver would search for a long time to beat the combination. And, in spite of our criticisms of the car, we don't think the improvements are as great as should have been made, we think Standard-Triumph has a real winner here." *Car and Driver* called it "the most important story to come out of England since the E-Type Jaguar."

This was one of the last times that Triumph was compared to Jaguar. At least until they were under the same roof. By 1961, Lyons and Jaguar had moved significantly upmarket with their design, features, and performance. One of the most triumphant moments in British sports car history would have to be the unveiling of the Jaguar XK-E. It was like nothing anyone had ever seen. The evolution of the E-Type carried on for more than 10 years and remains one of the greatest automotive designs.

All accolades aside, the TR4 was the last production model Alick Dick oversaw. Throughout most of his tenure at the head of Standard-Triumph, he was looking for a partner to help the company remain independent and, more important, afloat. The cash garnered from the Ferguson tractor sell-off was quickly gobbled up through the acquisition of component suppliers such as Mulliners. Cash-strapped, as always, Dick was desperate for a buyer. After prolonged, fruitless negotiations with Rootes, Rover, and several

CHAPTER 3: The Italian Job

The cockpit of the TR4 was a much more comfortable place to be than its predecessor. The drafty side curtains were replaced with taller doors and full-size roll-up windows. The fixed windshield eliminated any drafts coming from the front; however, it also eliminated the possibility of changing over to the great-looking smaller windscreens.

The TR4 dashboard features the same layout as the TR3 with the large Jaeger speedo and tach immediately behind the steering wheel. At the center of the newly designed panel were fuel, temperature, oil pressure, and amps. All other controls were moved to a central housing below the gauges. The optional overdrive was moved to a stalk on the steering column. The "fly off" parking brake on the right side of the tunnel was a carry-over from the TR3. An AM radio, as seen here, was optional. (Photo Courtesy Classic Car Garage)

others, Leyland Motors Ltd. swooped in and purchased Standard-Triumph in December 1960. The money matters had been resolved but Triumph's management style clashed with Leyland's like oil and water. A year later, Dick was out of a job; Stanley Markland replaced him in 1961. However, before leaving, Dick had started a "bomb" ticking.

Through the first three years, four months, and 40,000 units, the TR4 remained largely unchanged. Actually, only the U.S. market received updates in late 1962. This included replacing the austere painted dashboard with a walnut veneer that gave the cockpit a much richer feel. The other cosmetic, and functional, change was eliminating the hand-crank starter. The grille no longer had an opening for the crankshaft, but the dimple remained in the lower valance panel. By this time, it was rare to find someone trying to start a car by hand.

Under the skin, Girling supplied lighter brake calipers, the SU carburetors were ditched in favor of Zenith-Stromberg 175CDs and a smoother flowing intake manifold. The latter change was less about performance, which was unchanged, but rather a supply chain decision. The SUs returned in a few years' time.

EVOLUTION OF AN ICON: THE TR4A

By the time Triumph was finally ready to bring out a new model, more than 40,000 units were forged with 95 percent of the output destined for the U.S. market. During that period, the one recurring knock on the car was the rear suspension. The car had a reputation for a very hard ride because of the minimal rear wheel travel created by parts-bin engineering.

The MGB is likely the most ubiquitous British sport car ever produced. Debuting in 1962, the MGB and its variations, MGB GT, and MGC, were built for 18 years with more than 520,000 units sold. The "B" was a monocoque design, which Triumph struggled to achieve, powered by a 1,798-cc 4-cylinder producing 95 hp. This powerplant was an enlarged version of the B series engine from the MGA and would essentially be the only engine used until MG production ceased in 1980. (Photo Courtesy Classic Car Garage)

The radio and controls for the heater are somewhat crudely mounted ahead of the shifter. The bracing over the transmission tunnel and the exposed cables indicate that these were add-ons. Nevertheless, it worked very well for the application and everything was efficient and conveniently located for the driver.

The first TR4s were offered with a white-painted dash fascia with a black surround on the center gauges. A more upscale wood veneer was offered in the second year of production, again aimed at the U.S. market. The popularity of the wood look makes the white panel a rare sight. One of the biggest changes to the dash was the incorporation of air vents at the outer corners. (Photo Courtesy Classic Car Garage)

Car and Driver called the ride "choppy" and in a road test said, "If there is one important disadvantage in the TR4, it is certainly the design of the rear suspension." Triumph's somewhat pedestrian sedan, the Herald, had independent rear suspension (IRS) thanks to the transverse leaf spring setup. Further exacerbating the problem was the much smoother ride of the new MGB, introduced in 1962.

The problem was quickly solved by adapting the TR4 frame to carry the advanced rear suspension unit from the larger, more luxurious Triumph 2000 sedan.

The side frame rails were moved outward between the wheels and a special section was built at the rear crossmember to act as a hanger for the unit. Conspicuously large cast-aluminum semi-trailing arms pivoted at the frame and brake drums. The 2000's telescoping dampeners did not fit, so lever-arm dampeners were mounted transversely outboard of the differential on the supporting frame bridge. A large crossbeam sat atop the coil springs. Each half-shaft featured a splined version of a modern CV joint to handle wheel travel. Unfortunately, the splines had a tendency to jam when you put the spurs to it in first gear. This was remedied by regular maintenance and heavy application of axle grease.

The design and execution was brilliant. In 1965, *Autocar* said, "The greatest improvement in the TR undoubtedly comes from the rear suspension. Now the TR can be driven deliberately fast at obstacles it would have shied away from before." *Car and Driver* called the IRS a "considerable improvement" and noted that the ride was "fantastically improved." (The introduction of the IRS TR4A made

The view from the "other side": a right-hand-drive TR4 showing the wood veneer dashboard. The parking brake was always on the right side of the tunnel and thereby put all the controls on the right. It does not interfere with the driver despite the narrower footwell.

Triumph the only auto manufacturer with IRS in every production model.)

The most obvious cosmetic change was the chrome trim strip that ran from the doors forward and grew to house the turn-signal lights at the nose. The grille was revised and new chrome badges appeared on the trunk lid touting the IRS. At the nose, the 12-year-old TR shield was replaced by the Triumph globe.

The rest of the world finally received the upgrades that the Americans had been enjoying for years, including the

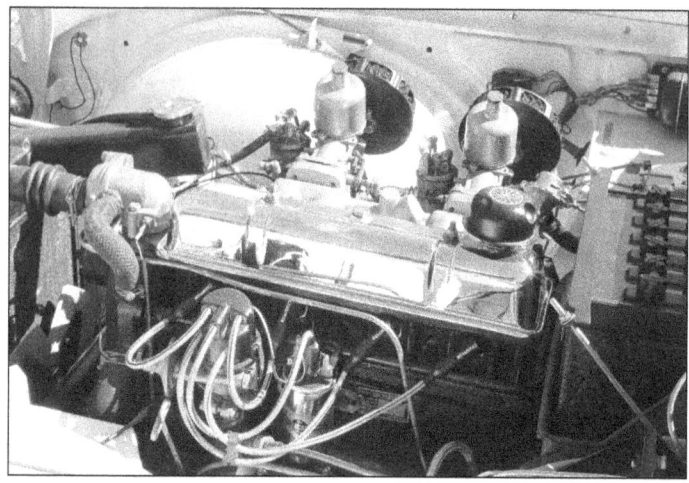

Everything under the hood was a direct carry-over from the predecessor except for the carburetor setup. A supply-chain decision put the old SUs on the shelf in favor of Zenith-Stromberg 175CD carburetors bolted to a slightly modified intake manifold. The SUs returned later on.

The increased space between the new wider grille and the front of the radiator required a tunnel of sorts to channel the incoming air directly into the cooling fins.

The TR4 received a mild cosmetic makeover in 1965 and was introduced as the TR4-A. The factory brochure showcased a host of upgrades for the TR4-A, including the wood-veneer dashboard with the fresh-air vent featured prominently. Externally, the chief differences were the full-width horizontal bars in the grille that replaced the old mesh-style look and front-fender marker lamps accentuated by a chrome flash running rearward across the doors. Wire wheels were an option as were white-wall tires. That combination was definitely a 1960s-era look. (Photo Courtesy Author Collection)

Additional changes included a chrome TR4-A badge that adorned the lower trunk-lid face. The image of the woman putting the convertible top into place suggests that it's a simple one-handed affair. Although the new design made it a little easier to operate the convertible top than on the TR3, it was not as simple as the Mazda Miata of today. (Photo Courtesy Author Collection)

This original press photo shows the cosmetic differences at the rear of the new model, including the TR-4A and IRS script along with the new dual exhaust pipes. Also shown here are the accents for being a thoroughly mod 1960s couple, replete with sunglasses and string-back driving gloves. And let's not forget the Pall Malls. (Photo Courtesy *Car and Driver*)

This press photo highlights the chrome flash running the length of the front half of the car. Also shown here are the optional 48-spoke knock-off wire wheels with optional white-wall tires. Very hip for the times. (Photo Courtesy *Car and Driver*)

The TR250 (TR5) introduced in 1968. I think it's the best of the breed. The handsome good looks of Michelotti's handiwork are coupled with the bigger, stronger 2.5-liter 6-cylinder engine.

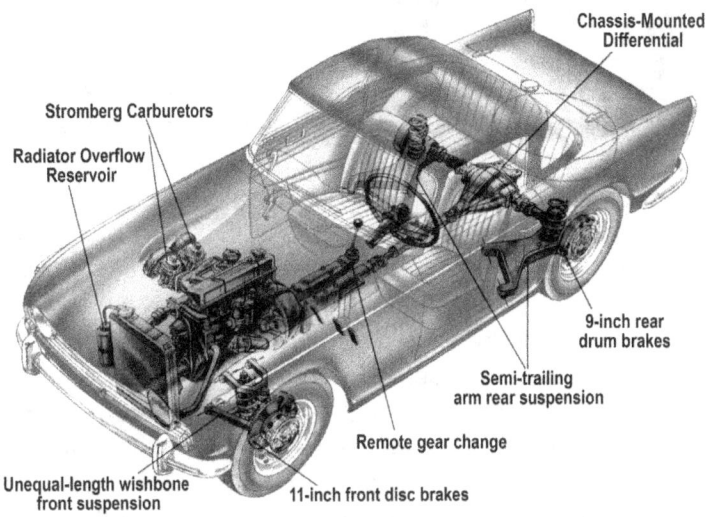

The most significant change to the TR4A was the introduction of optional independent rear suspension (IRS). Through its first four years, the knock on the TR4 was its handling and choppy ride. The solution was to adopt the rear suspension setup from the 2000 sedan. A large cross beam was mounted atop coil springs to handle suspension travel and splined half-shafts transmitted power to the wheels.

The new TR4A IRS allowed Triumph to boast that it was the only manufacturer with IRS available in every production model. (Photo Courtesy *Car and Driver*)

walnut-veneer dashboard, improved seat padding, sun visors, and a new grille. The handbrake finally moved from the footwell to the top of the transmission tunnel, and headlights and overdrive were actuated by stalks on the steering column. Neighbors of TR owners were appeased by splitting the single exhaust pipe at the center of the car and installing twin mufflers with dual outlet pipes.

Unbelievably, just as Triumph thought its problems were solved and it had distanced itself from the "underslung" label of the 1950s, the U.S. dealer network balked at the new design. They were selling TR4s on the merits of price and performance and felt that the IRS, which put the price over $3,000, caused too much of a price barrier. Because the U.S. market was so important, the factory created a less costly, live-axle version solely for the United States. Triumph was able to use the new chassis and fashion a solid rear axle system using semi-elliptic leaf springs in place of the large coil springs.

The IRS version weighed nearly 2,240 pounds while the live-axle car tipped the scales at 2,211 pounds. In either

TR250/TR5: TRIUMPH'S POPULAR CAR BECOMES MORE POTENT

This view of the frame illustrates the wider bell shape ahead of the new rear suspension mounting. Although heavier and clunky by today's standards, the IRS improved the handling of the TR4 dramatically. In a happy accident, the greater width and strength of the redesigned frame allowed for an easy transplant of the inline 6-cylinder engine.

case, the car was heavier than the 2,128 pounds of the original TR4 and everything from new sleeves to no sleeves was tried to wring more power out of the 2,138-cc engine. Nothing could be done to offset the additional ballast that caused a decline in performance. The TR4A gave up a second in the quarter-mile and nearly as much in 0-60–mph time. The time-tested, wet-sleeve Vanguard 4-cylinder had reached the end of its useful life. In July 1967, the last TR4A rolled off the Coventry assembly line and the sporting life of the wet-sleeve powerplant came to a close.

The late 1960s ushered in a host of changes. As the TR line cried out for a new powerplant, the U.S. government imposed new safety and pollution laws. Triumph engineers were now saddled with marketing's demands as well as conforming to federal government mandates.

The first thing that needed to be addressed was performance. The horsepower gains in the 4A were not enough to overcome the additional weight. Conveniently, one of the interesting byproducts of the revised TR4A frame was that the increased width and strength could easily accommodate the 2-liter 6-cylinder engine from the 2000 sedan.

The frame also had provision for a bulkier automatic transmission, of which two prototypes were built. The cars were tested in the United States, but were summarily dismissed in short order. (After all, the MG automatic was such a disaster, why would Triumph even spend the money?)

Yes, the new 6-cylinder was essentially the same displacement as the 4-cylinder it was replacing. But it was a smoother-running engine and the power was scalable whereas the 4-cylinder wet-sleeve mill had reached its limit. However, there was another issue.

Although the 1,998-cc 6-cylinder engine fit nicely under the hood and weighed roughly the same as the 4-cylinder, it actually offered less torque and less horsepower than the 2.2-liter engine it was replacing. Cylinder bore could not be increased but stroke could, so it was lengthened from 76 to 95 mm. A bonus to this unusually long stroke was that it also increased torque dramatically. A redesigned block and cylinder head with larger combustion chambers, coupled with

Just as Triumph was rolling out its 6-cylinder models, production on the Austin-Healey 3000 was coming to an end. Donald Healey had recognized that there was an opportunity in the market for a sports car with greater performance and more niceties than Triumph or MG but for less money than Jaguar. The initial Austin-Healey 100-4 was offered with a 2,660-cc inline 4-cylinder with 90 hp. Named "100" for its top speed, it was the first of the cars to be dubbed a "Big Healey" to differentiate from the smaller Sprites. In 1956, a 2,639-cc engine was offered and the designation became 100-6. The wheelbase was lengthened and a 2+2 seat was offered. By 1959, the displacement was bumped to 2,912 cc and rebranded "3000." The Mark 3 version introduced in 1963 made 150 hp and featured a nicely appointed cockpit. The Austin-Healey line of sports cars was offered by BMC from 1955 through 1967. (Photo Courtesy Classic Car Garage)

On the outside, the new TR250 was easily identified by the racing stripe draped across the front of the hood and wrapping across the front fenders. These kinds of unique graphics, racing stripes typically ran longitudinally, were quite popular at the time in the United States.

The TR250 (or TR5) wasn't exactly a wolf in sheep's clothing, but the fact that it carried over the cleaner horizontal grille bars and side-marker lamps from the TR4A belies what is under the hood. Only the badges on the hood and trunk gave it away. This was particularly evident in Britain, where the fuel-injected version produced nearly 50 more horsepower than the dual-carb TR4A.

the increased stroke, produced a 2,498-cc engine rated at 104 hp.

Obviously, a new model with a larger engine that only put out 104 horses would never do. At that time, Lucas Electrical Company was working on a new mechanical fuel-injection system. Triumph saw this as a multi-faceted opportunity. The improved fuel delivery made it possible to run a much hotter camshaft. It was also hoped that the fuel injection would make it easier to comply with the new U.S. emissions requirements.

But the good news, in Great Britain anyway, was that the TR5 was released in October 1968. The new car was powered by the 2.5-liter fuel-injected 6-cylinder that pumped out 150 hp with 164 ft-lbs of torque. Despite a 50-percent improvement in output, the car weighed only 28 pounds more than the 4A. This was the kind of performance increase that Triumph needed to regain its position as the low-cost performance sports car.

The new horses were harnessed by the same front-disc/rear-drum layout. Because of the extra power, a servo was now standard along with a dual-pot master cylinder. Enthu-

siasts will recognize the debut of the "modern" clear plastic cap on the new master cylinder. In addition, the fly-off parking brake was discontinued for the first time in a TR model.

On the outside, the distinctive hood bulge was retained despite being made redundant by the fuel-injection system. The popular Redline Michelin tires were offered along with the faux mag wheel hubcaps known as Rostyle wheel covers. The wheel covers were fitted to all cars delivered with the standard 4½-inch-wide steel wheels; they were frequently the target of motoring journalists who found them to be poorly conceived.

The interior was largely unchanged from the previous model. The seats were contoured to be more like bucket seats than individual little benches, and trimmed with white piping. The door panels and rear surrounds were also trimmed with more deluxe-looking vinyl.

On top of the performance gains, Triumph was also able to boast the first fuel-injected mass-produced car in Britain. While the fuel injection system delivered great power and was something for Triumph marketers to crow about, it was not without its issues. The biggest problem was that the

A TR250 badge, TR5 in the rest of the world, was placed off-center near the front edge of the hood. A TR250 badge also appeared on the trunk lid. (TR5 Photo Courtesy John Allen)

The 1,998-cc 6-cylinder that was originally brought over from the 2000 sedan fit nicely. However, it produced less horsepower and torque than the 2.2-liter engine it was replacing. The fix was to lengthen the stroke and add a new Lucas fuel (petrol) injection (FI) system. These modifications resulted in an exhilarating 150 hp and 164 ft-lbs of torque.

system required a steady pressure of 100 psi, and when the fuel tank ran low, the system could not maintain adequate pressure, which caused a bad case of chuggle, or surging.

There was a lot of fanfare for the new model, but much to the disappointment of American TR enthusiasts, emissions legislation prevented the TR5 from coming Stateside. To pass the emissions standards, Triumph would have had to modify the injection system extensively and everyone

The beautifully presented and far more stimulating fuel-injected TR5 powerplant. Rated at 150 hp and 164 ft-lbs of torque, this was the performance upgrade that Triumph wanted for its new model. The cars ran very strong and were a joy to drive, but the Lucas system was finicky to keep in tune. (Photo Courtesy Classic Car Garage)

Unfortunately for the United States, the Lucas FI system could not meet the new anti-smog regulations and a carbureted version was the only option for Triumph. The stroked 2.5-liter with carburetors made just 104 hp. It was smoother and more tractable than the 4-cylinder, but just 104 hp was a disappointment. A stifling air-intake box was fitted over the dual carbs; PCV tubing can be seen. (Photo Courtesy Classic Car Garage)

knows how adverse it was to spending money. Even then, there would be no guarantee that the modifications would pass the new regulations. In the end, it had to drop the fuel injection and return to carburetors. Twin Stromberg 175CDs were fitted along with a more pedestrian cam profile to produce a far less exciting, but still reasonably potent, 104 hp at 4,500 rpm and 143 ft-lbs of torque. Named for the 2.5-liter displacement, the TR250 was born.

The only differences between the two cars were how the fuel was delivered and some external badging. The 250 is also easily distinguished by the racing stripe draped across the end of the hood and front fenders. A small TR250 badge was affixed off-center near the front lip of the hood. The live rear axle was dead, and both models were available with only the IRS carried over from the 4A. The U.S. models also received slightly wider rubber all around.

International symbols adorned the new switches to illustrate what they controlled. The high polish was gone from the wooden fascia in favor of a more natural look and fully gimbaled round vents replaced the old squarish vents.

Despite some of the foibles of the Lucas injection system, the TR5 was far more exhilarating to drive. It was a bonafide 120-mph sports car capable of 0-60–mph times of just over 8 seconds. The TR5 covered the quarter-mile in 16.5 seconds.

Contrast that with the TR250's 10.6 seconds to 60 mph and a quarter-mile time of 17.9 seconds. *Road & Track* coaxed 107 mph out of the 250 while *Motor* reported a top speed of 117 mph for the TR5. At $3,795, the TR250 compared favorably with the E-Type at $6,000. *Road & Track's* test summary said it best, "Offsetting the TR250's new-found powerplant smoothness and interior conveniences is a body structure well behind modern standards in terms of strength and resistance to rattles. An entirely new model would have been more exciting to us."

As it turns out, plans were already underway to replace the aging body design. The TR250/5 had a brief run of just 15 months. Production ended in September 1968 with 8,484 TR250s and 2,947 TR5s built. All of the TR250s were exported to North America while the fuel-injected TR5s were sold in Britain and Europe.

Once again, another one got away with the TR250/TR5. The handsome good looks of Michelotti's TR4 matched with a larger powerplant made the car even more fun to drive. Unfortunately, U.S. federal regulations prevented the American market from enjoying the true potential of the car. Triumph was unable to deliver smog-legal performance and the aging body-on-frame was showing its cracks.

When reading a book about your favorite cars, the last thing you want to get into is meetings, mergers, and corporate politics. However, it's important to note what was happening to Triumph at this important point in its history because it set the course for all future decisions and model development. Leyland was firmly in control of Triumph by this time and, despite all its best efforts and strong sales, Triumph was still showing a loss.

At about this time in 1968, Leyland merged with British Motor Holdings (formerly BMC) to form British Leyland Motor Corporation. In doing so it brought all of Britain's greatest sports car marques under one roof. It's difficult to believe that the merger made financial sense, but it was at a time in Britain when mergers of this type were not uncommon. The idea was to combine an unhealthy company with a solid company to shore up the flailing company. It did not work. As a result, the once sworn enemies of MG and Triumph now shared resources and oversight along with Jaguar, Austin, and Rover.

From this point forward the decisions on development, or lack of development, across a huge range of cars were based more on accounting than engineering. There was one pool of resources to divide across a host of cars, all of which were sorely in need of development. The deck was stacked against them from the beginning.

The cockpit layout was unchanged but featured nicer appointments, a more highly polished wood veneer, padded seats with accent piping, and gimbaled "eyeball" air vents. The floor-mounted parking brake was relocated to the top of the transmission tunnel between the seats.

CHAPTER 4

WHAT BEGAN IN GERMANY RETURNS TO GERMANY

The new TR6 marked a milestone because it was the first Triumph since 1958 that wasn't designed by Giovanni Michelotti. The new body design was penned by Gerhart Giesecke of Karmann in Osnabruck, West Germany. (Photo Courtesy Classic Car Garage)

The TR6 was the last of a breed for Triumph and maybe the last of the quintessential sports car breed all together. Everything about the car embodied the character of British sports car lore: chiseled good looks, brute-like torque, steering wheel in your chest, and gobs of air-through-the-hair open-car fun. It was every clichéd sports car superlative you can think of on four wheels.

When the TR6 was introduced in January 1969 it was the result of yet another rush-to-market by Triumph. It desperately wanted to replace the body-on-frame design but had not worked far enough ahead to anticipate a completely new design. Once again, when Triumph needed it most, the company could afford it least. It did not have the capacity to produce new tooling and to top it off, Michelotti, whom Triumph had relied on for more than a decade, had so many projects going that he could not help. He offered a quick rendering, but it was never seriously considered.

There was no going back because the venerable 2.2-liter wet-sleeve Vanguard engine had outlived its usefulness and the 2.5-liter replacement was a diamond in the rough that needed polishing. Triumph was scrambling, but as it turned out, help came from an unlikely source.

Technical director Harry Webster had heard that German coachbuilder Wilhelm Karmann of Osnabruck, West Germany, was expanding and looking for work. Karmann is best known and most closely associated with its designs for Volkswagen; not only the Beetle, but its namesake, the Karmann Ghia. However, Karmann also built cars for Ford, BMW, and Porsche.

Late in 1967, Karmann was given the seemingly impossible task of designing a new car on a limited budget within 15 months. Karmann wanted the project badly enough to volunteer to provide some of the required tooling, and Triumph was in no position to turn this down. The real catch was that the new car had to retain the same structure and use as many existing parts as possible. This meant that the center area of the car specifically, the most expensive to retool, could not be modified. It was a familiar challenge for every designer that worked with Triumph.

Given that the area between the wheels was off-limits, stylist Gerhart Giesecke concentrated on the front and rear. His design gave the illusion of an entirely new car and completely disguised the fact that it was sitting on the same old, narrow frame.

The chiseled, handsome good looks of the TR6 were accentuated by the revised rear panel of the new design and the taller, more aggressive 15-inch wheels. Once again, the masterful design work created a bold new car that looked nothing like its predecessor but was built directly from it. (Photo Courtesy Classic Car Garage)

Once again, through the magic of the stylist's pen, the new car looked bigger and wider than its predecessor. The long flat hood, wider grille, flared fenders, and re-sculpted rear flanks gave the TR6 a mightier and masculine look. (Photo Courtesy Classic Car Garage)

The rear of the car looked longer and wider thanks to the German-style flat rear panel known as the Kamm-tail. The trunk lid latched at the top of the vertical panel, which meant a higher lift for placing parcels into the expanded storage cavity. The new design provided 6.1 cubic feet of space, an 8-percent increase over the TR4. (Photo Courtesy Classic Car Garage)

The masculine look of the car was re-enforced by flattening all panels and deleting any unnecessary trim elements. The aggressive-looking stance was achieved by moving the headlights all the way out to the edges of the grille and using a narrower, full-width radiator opening. The hood was completely flat except where it rose to meet the fenders; the carburetor bulge was removed.

The rear of the car looked longer and wider thanks to the use of the trademark German flat rear panel known as a Kamm-tail design. The name comes from designer and aerodynamicist Wunibald Kamm who created the truncated rear design to reduce turbulence at high speeds. It's frequently been said that the German designers don't know how to end a car. This may be the origin of that assessment; just cut it off where it makes sense.

Like it or not, the new design resulted in increased luggage space: from 5.6 to 6.1 cubic feet. The vertical cathedral-style taillamps of the TR4 were replaced with horizontally mounted rectangular lights that wrapped around to the rear fenders slightly. It was a stylish way to comply with the need for side-marker lights in the United States. It was decided that the rear panel should be painted black regardless of the body color. Restored cars frequently have this panel painted gloss black and although it looks nicer, it is

CHAPTER 4: What Began in Germany Returns to Germany

The overall front of the new design was taller than the previous car but looked sleeker thanks to the full-width but narrower grille. The TR6 badge fit nicely into the horizontal center bar. The optional black-plastic chin spoiler was a popular add-on that first appeared in 1973.

The elegant cathedral taillights were replaced with modern, square wraparound lights that were more complementary to the new design. It was also a cleaner solution for incorporating the side-marker lights that were becoming mandatory.

not correct. U.S.-bound models also received outlined TR6 lettering on each rear flank, which harkens to the Pontiac GTO trim of the same period.

Giesecke achieved the new look through minimums: minimal curves, minimal chrome, and minimal badging. This is a significant departure from all previous TR models. The only chrome on the car was the one-piece front and rear bumpers, door handles, and headlight trim rings. Badging was reduced to a rectangle at the center of the grille mounted on a chrome spear that bisected the black egg-crate pattern. A small Triumph nameplate appeared on the upper right corner of the crisply cleaned-up rear panel. In the British market, the left-hand corner of the rear panel wore a badge touting "Fuel Injection," which was replaced with an "Overdrive" badge for cars headed to the American market. Symmetry.

SIX APPEAL

Giesecke's ever-so-gentle flaring of the wheel arches gave the illusion of a wider stance. It also allowed for a 5½-inch-wide wheel that also helped contribute to the wider appearance. The 175-15 Michelin radial tires filled out the wheelwells beautifully. The much-maligned Rostyle wheel covers were standard equipment; painted 72-spoke wire wheels were an option. An anti-roll bar was also added to the front suspension.

The car was essentially the TR5/250 beneath all the new sheet metal and in the cockpit. The flat-finish wooden fascia remained unchanged, except for modest differences in markings on the instruments and a different hue marking the redline.

Karmann's crisper, almost square lines gave the TR6 a bigger, more powerful stance. The angular elements of the design are accentuated with the factory hardtop in place. (Photo Courtesy David Gooley)

When the car bowed upon its entrance in 1968, the carbureted (U.S. market) version of the four-main-bearing 2.5-liter produced 104 bhp and 153 ft-lbs of torque; the fuel-injected model (British market) delivered a more raucous 150 bhp and 164 ft-lbs of torque. The same all-synchro 4-speed box propelled the car forward and the same front-disc/rear-drum brake layout arrested the TR6 from speed. The optional Laycock de Normanville overdrive was operational in three forward speeds.

Whether fuel injected or carbureted, the TR6 has one undeniable trait: that unmistakable exhaust note. The tailpipes deliver the perfect growl with just the right amount

The redesigned car was still a Triumph and that meant a full-on, wind-in-your-hair sports car, so a tonneau cover was part of the package. The same concept dated back to the first TR and allowed the driver to button up half of the cockpit to reduce excess draft and the elements. It was still an era when locking your car wasn't such a big thing so the car could be parked with full tonneau in place.

Despite the center section of the tub being unchanged from the previous design, the new interior appointments were much more luxurious in appearance. From door to door, everything was more integrated and that included full carpets and redesigned seats with better bolstering and taller backs. (Photo Courtesy Classic Car Garage)

It's difficult to improve on a winning design. The speedometer and rev count remained the largest instruments mounted ahead of the drive while the supplemental monitoring meters were mounted in the center. More modern rocker-style switches were incorporated into the ever-popular wood-veneer dash.

Overall, the cockpit of the TR6 became more civilized. The refinements included better carpet, taller reclining seatbacks with lateral support, and better finishing on the cluster over the transmission tunnel. The bracing supported the radio and helped shore up the dashboard to reduce scuttle shudder. The locking glove box and the gimbaled round vents remained a constant throughout the TR6 production run. (Photo Courtesy Brian Wyka)

Anti-theft regulations required Triumph to add a locking steering column to all models. The easiest way to accomplish this was to relocate the tumbler assembly under the dash adjacent to the steering column. It was effective from the anti-theft point of view, but drivers found the placement and operation awkward and unnatural.

The U.S. version of the 2.5-liter four-main-bearing inline 6. Early versions of the TR6 were rated at 106 hp. Unfortunately U.S. emissions legislation prevented any meaningful performance development to this engine and horsepower dropped to 104. (Photo Courtesy David Gooley)

The dual Stromberg carburetors fed the horizontal manifold to deliver a top speed of 110 mph and a 0-60–time in the mid-11-second range. The 133 ft-lbs of torque did not snap necks, but it did help deliver the well-documented TR rear-end squat. When launching off the line, the rear suspension compresses and causes significant negative camber at the rear wheels. (Photo Courtesy David Gooley)

The fuel-injected version of the 2.5-liter engine produced a far more robust 150 hp, which made for a more meaningful driving experience. This example is enhanced with braided hoses and a polished-aluminum valvecover. (Photo Courtesy Classic Car Garage)

of burble and not too overpowering when you wind it to redline. It says that this is a real sports car.

The new TR sat on coil springs and telescopic dampeners up front and the tried-and-true semi-trailing arm independent suspension at the rear. This suspension layout and the high torque output contributed to "rear-end squat." When launching the car from stop or running it hard from first to second gear, the rear suspension compressed all the way to the stops. While this phenomenon certainly contributed to the feeling of power, it was actually taking energy away from acceleration and many owners found it annoying. It was finally rectified with the 1971 models when Triumph fitted stiffer rear springs. Perhaps this was a bone of contention at the time, but today's enthusiasts find that it's a kick-in-the-pants reminder of the TR6's brute torque.

The base price at the time of introduction was $3,300 or £1,000. Options included wire wheels, overdrive, tonneau cover, seatbelts, and a radio. This compared favorably to the competition; the MGC cost $4,300 and the MGB cost $3,000. In comparison, the Jensen-Healey cost $4,500, the Morgan

Throughout its history, Triumph's marketing connected on-track success with the production models. Here at the 1975 Liverpool Motor Show, Bob Tullius' Group 44 TR6 is showcased alongside a production model. Tullius' impeccably prepared cars were highlighted by the iconic white livery with Quaker State sponsorship. Behind the production TR6 is a Stag; on the far side is a Dolomite sedan. (Photo Courtesy British Motor Industry Heritage Trust)

Plus 8 cost $4,900, and the Sunbeam Tiger cost $3,800. The TR6's chief competition would have been the Austin-Healey 3000, which had ceased production the previous year.

The 2.5-liter engine remained unchanged throughout the life of the TR6 with the exception of more and more power-robbing modifications heaped upon it by U.S. emissions laws. A revised engine would have been too costly so Triumph made improvements where it could, but power never went up. Only down. Other manufacturers couldn't cope and eventually their cars, including the Jaguar E-Type, Lotus Elan, Saab Sonnet, and Opel GT, succumbed to the ever-emasculating regulations.

Unfortunately, the bugs were never really worked out of the fuel injection to allow it to be used in the United States and the dual Strombergs prevailed until the end. By adjusting fuel flow, compression ratio, and camshafts, Triumph was able to maintain 105 hp on the U.S. model, even with the air pump, in 1976. But torque suffered and it was badly missed by anyone looking for that sports car feel. The "American" TR6 was rated at 133 ft-lbs of torque while its fuel-injected sibling boasted 143 ft-lbs. The rest of the world also enjoyed the more exhilarating performance of the 150 hp from the injected version.

The enthusiastic media cheered the new look but recognized the car for what it was. "As it stands, the TR6 does offer a distinctive combination of qualities at a reasonable price: a traditional British sports car package with ride and

The TR6 was the last of the cars with any sort of lineage connecting it to the original Triumph sports cars. It was also the most popular of all the models to date with more than 94,000 sold. More than 86,000 of those were exported to the United States. This early version shows the Rostyle wheel covers, complete with faux chrome lug nuts. These wheel covers were originally introduced with the TR4A and also came on the GT6. They were not popular and were frequently replaced. (Photo Courtesy British Motor Industry Heritage Trust)

CHAPTER 4: What Began in Germany Returns to Germany

There are two common denominators throughout the history of Triumph's sports cars: short on time and short of capital. Yet somehow each successive car bested the previous model in style and appeal. The TR6 was no exception. The stunning design completely masked the fact that the center tub and many chassis components carried forward from the TR250. (Photo Courtesy Classic Car Garage)

handling far from outstanding and a somewhat cramped cockpit but, off-setting there, an excellent 6-cylinder engine, luxurious finish and trimmings, and a roadster top that's easy to put up and down," said Road & Track. Autocar praised the fuel-injected version for performance and price but criticized the harsh ride, calling it "taut and joggly."

The U.S.-spec version could reach 60 mph from rest in 10.7 seconds against the fuelie version's 8.2 seconds. They covered the quarter-mile in 17.9 seconds and 16.3 seconds, respectively.

Although the TR6 remained largely unchanged during its eight-year run, the rush to market in 1969 left a number of details that needed attention. Although many of these items are subtle, they are of value to the enthusiast and help the novice tell the cars apart.

In 1970, reclining seats were added. American safety laws required U.S.-bound cars to have headrests, and the ignition switch was relocated below the dash to provide the mandated steering lock mechanism. It was an extremely unpopular change and proved to be somewhat awkward to operate. The Rostyle wheels were discontinued in favor of a painted steel wheel with a black center hub adorned with TR6 lettering. Twin exhaust pipes were added in late 1971 for the 1972 model year.

A flat-black chin spoiler was added in 1973 and the wire wheel option was dropped in favor of chrome trim rings. The

Triumph, actually British Leyland, sponsored the popular television series M*A*S*H in the 1970s. Subsequently, Alan Alda owned a TR6 and was part of the promotional campaign. Horsepower remained stuck at a disappointing 104 and was the only specification not cited on the back of the brochure. (Photo Courtesy Author Collection)

center wheel hub changed from matte black to silver, matching the rest of the wheel. On the rear fenders, the TR6 emblem was melded with the Union Jack on all U.S.-bound cars.

The U.S. emissions regulations had forced an emasculated engine on American TR-lovers, but when U.S. safety regulations forced rubber bumper overriders onto the cars in 1974, it was adding insult to injury. To meet bumper height minimums, shims were put in the springs to raise the car and the signal lights were mounted below the bumpers. Further safety laws required an ignition lock-out if seatbelts were not fastened prior to starting the car. One positive note was that overdrive was now a standard feature.

By 1976, Father Time had, unfortunately, caught up with the TR6. The design of the chassis was now more than 15 years old and anti-pollution regulations had sapped the life out of the 2.5-liter engine; it could no longer deliver enough performance to offset the burgeoning weight. At 2,438 pounds, 105 hp was not enough to get noticed in the face of new competition from the Datsun 260Z, which delivered 150 hp at the same weight.

The demise of the TR6 was the first sports car casualty under British Leyland, which took over Standard-Triumph just as the TR6 was being developed. It wasn't as though British Leyland ignored the TR6, it just left well-enough alone and maintained the car with minimal investment. The aforementioned accounting issues deemed the costs of making the necessary improvements too high. British Leyland was more interested in updating its manufacturing and with it an entirely new TR model.

July 1976 marked the end of an era as the last true TR rolled off the line and headed for America. It was just shy of a quarter century after Sir John Black's first TR2s were produced. Other than the very private Morgan, sports cars would no longer be designed in this way. More TR6s were sold than any other TR model to date.

By 1973, U.S. safety regulations required better crash protection on all cars. British Leyland's answer was to install large, rubber bumper overriders on all models. Triumphs, MGs, and Jaguars all received these large appendages. To meet the new minimum bumper heights, shims were put in the springs to raise the ride height of the car. The addition of a Union Jack to the TR6 emblem was also new for 1974.

By 1975, the TR6 had become the most successful TR model in Triumph history. When production gave way to the TR7 in 1976, more than 94,000 TR6s had been sold. This also illustrates the advancements in manufacturing techniques since the TR3s were produced. (Photo Courtesy British Motor Industry Heritage Trust)

CHAPTER 4: What Began in Germany Returns to Germany

CHAPTER 5

SEVENTH HEAVEN: TRIUMPH GETS A WEDGIE

When the TR7 was unveiled in 1975, it was not like any model that preceded it. No part of the TR6 was carried over to the new platform. Unlike any other TR model, it featured a unibody design and was only available as a coupe. No convertible was initially offered; in fact, a convertible version was not offered until 1979. (Photo Courtesy Simon Goldsworthy/Triumph World)

Whenever the TR7 comes up in conversation the first thing you get is the eye roll. Sometimes it's the knowing smirk of displeasure and people of a certain age may recite the introductory advertising slogan, "The shape of things to come." And even that is said in a sarcastic manner.

Unfortunately the Wedge cars are synonymous with the downfall of Triumph and therefore not appreciated as they should be. True, they were unlike any of the previous cars in the line. True, they had production and quality issues in the early days of the launch. True, they were the very last cars to carry the TR badge. Despite all of this, they are indeed good cars and deserving of serious consideration.

It is a little ironic that if you were to invert the triangle-shaped graphic that accompanied the advertising slogan it would closely replicate a steeply declining sales graph that many associate with the last TRs. This may have been the ultimate reality, however. At one point in its production, more TR7s were sold than any TR model before it.

After the TR6 was rushed to market, plans for an all-new TR model were already in the works at the time the British Leyland–British Motor Company merger took place in 1968. The new car, code named Bullet, was to be a completely new design aimed at the United States first and the rest of the world second. This was to be the first new TR developed without any pre-existing conditions, and that included engine stipulations or frame and body panel restrictions. The Bullet was also being designed completely in-house.

Once again, unibody construction was planned from the start, but this time it was not abandoned as it had been in the past. Designing a new car for the U.S. market meant meeting the ever-tightening EPA and safety regulations. By this time, requirements included side-impact beams in the door, roll-over protection, minimum headlight height restrictions, and crash-resistant 5-mph bumpers. Triumph, again fearing the unknown, felt that there was enough momentum behind the mounting roll-over laws that the U.S. regulations would outlaw the convertible altogether.

Hindsight is always 20-20 and you might scoff at their fear, but who could blame them? Most American car manufacturers were eliminating convertibles from their lineups. However, this was due less to the impending government regulations and more to declining sales.

Americans wanted more comfort and convertibles took a hit with the advent of the reliable power sunroof. In a few short years the removable glass panels, known as "T-Tops" became all the rage. These indicators quickly led the Bullet project to become a fixed-head (hardtop) coupe. A removable roof panel was also under consideration so that the Triumph could still be an open-air sports car. Eventually, one was offered.

Despite the promise of no restrictions dictating the new design, it didn't take long for the new management to start

Testing the TR7 prototype in Wales with Tony Lee (passenger) and John Lloyd (driver). To disguise the actual shape of the car from spy shots, fins were added to the tops of the fenders and some of the trim was deleted. The test car featured the optional sunroof. As can be seen by the rugged terrain in the background, this was an extreme conditions test. (Photo Courtesy Moss Motors)

After years of consideration and concepts, Triumph finally installed pop-up headlamps. One of Michelotti's concepts for the Spitfire featured pop-up headlamps but the idea was scrapped for fear of the United States outlawing the feature in the name of safety.

Billed as "the shape of things to come," the car was distinctly angular from front, rear, and profile views. Everything about the design was in response to ever-stricter impact legislation in the United States. Stronger sills and a crush-proof tub were required. The delicate chrome bumpers of the TR6 gave way to larger, black impact-absorbing units. Bumpers were black regardless of the body color. (Photo Courtesy Simon Goldsworthy/Triumph World)

looking for economies. At about this time the MGC was dropped after a short three-plus-year run. The 6-cylinder GTs and convertibles never found their mark, but the TR6 continued to thrive. Somewhere, MGC enthusiasts are bemoaning a British Leyland accountant's decision.

At the same time, a great deal of energy and resources were being poured into the launch of the new V-12 Jaguar XJ sedans. The world's only mass-produced V-12 (as claimed in advertising) was experiencing significant teething problems because the cars overheated easily. The 5.3-liter 12-cylinder was shoehorned into the too-small engine bay, which left little room for airflow or even a mechanic's fingers, for that matter.

It's easy to see that the division of resources became an issue. Down the very same hall, the MG design contingent was asked to explore a new mid-engine concept. During the 1970s, mid-engine designs were a constant, but few ever saw production. The early 1970s were also about hatchbacks, so Triumph was asked to look at a 2+2 hatchback version of the Bullet sports car. This idea had more legs than the mid-engine suggestion because these designs were selling well in the United States. Chevrolet was promoting its new Vega, Ford was getting ready to roll out with the Pinto, and Honda and Toyota were growing rapidly in popularity.

This original Leyland release shows a cutaway of the forthcoming TR7. Note that it was not to be released to the public until January 1975. The schematic shows the slant-4 and the intertwined air and cooling hoses. This illustration also shows the sliding canvas top. (Photo Courtesy Author Collection)

A prototype called Lynx was a 2+2 hatchback based on the new Bullet concepts. It went as far as a full-size model being built, but the project was eventually dropped. An MG version of the Bullet was also considered as the way to get a four-seat hatchback into production, but eventually Triumph was given all of the capital for a new car and MG was left to produce whatever it could on a shoestring budget. Many MG aficionados would say that British Leyland always shined a more favorable light on Triumph and MG development was always given short shrift. It's a difficult point to argue, but history seems to favor the theory. In truth there was very little capital to go around.

Originally code named Bullet, the TR7 platform was aimed squarely at the U.S. market. Because of this, a prototype hatchback version was considered and built. Code named Lynx, the concept was built but never pursued. (Photo Courtesy British Motor Industry Heritage Trust)

THE SHAPE OF THINGS

From the start of the Bullet project all of Triumph's styling exercises had

Stricter safety legislation also required energy-absorbing steering wheels. The result was a large pad at the center of the wheel giving a decidedly non–sports car appearance. Subsequent versions, such as this one, were not much better. Most owners replaced the wheel with a more appropriate version. (Photo Courtesy Author Collection)

The new car was powered by the 1,998-cc slant-4 that came from Leyland's supply to Saab. Dual Stromberg carburetors fed the 92-hp unit that was canted by 45 degrees to fit under the hood. The smaller 4-cylinder was chosen because it was certain to pass anti-pollution requirements.

The slant-4 wasn't a particularly handsome mill. Typically, cars with multiple carburetors are something to look at, but this was not the case. The excess anti-smog equipment and oversized air box are not becoming.

been founded on the wedge shape. Harris Mann, a Bertone fan from the Austin-Morris styling office, penned his version of the car based on the Italian show cars of the day. The car was to be strictly a two-seater with just enough room behind the seats for an odds-and-ends shelf. Interestingly, these same words described the TR2 concepts from 20 years earlier.

The wedge-shape coupe design was approved unanimously by British Leyland executives but is said to have lost some of its sizzle when it was adapted for production and U.S. regulations. Some of the sketches that float around today show a more rakish but sporting design that would have looked more like it came from the drawing boards of Mattel for the Hot Wheel toy cars.

With the approved body concept in hand, the next order of business was to mate it with the appropriate powerplant.

Rover had just been absorbed into the family and designers experimented with the 6-cylinder mill from the sedans. Even the little V-8s from the Rover lineup were under consideration. However, none of these engines could be made U.S. smog-legal without substantial investment and a negative impact on power output. Ultimately, in a surprising move, the Triumph 2.0-liter slant-4 was chosen for the new model. It is more surprising in hindsight because launching an entirely new car with a smaller, less-powerful engine than its predecessor does not make logical marketing sense.

The engine was the single overhead cam (SOHC) aluminum-head 1,998-cc unit that Triumph had been building for Saab's 99 models. Its 8.0:1 compression was fed by dual Stromberg carbs delivering 92 hp at 5,000 rpm and 115 ft-lbs of torque at 3,500 rpm. In a sense, it was picked by default because it was the only option that could easily meet EPA regulations and deliver 25 mpg to the economy-conscious target market while running an air conditioning compressor and air pump. And don't forget the need to run the new unleaded fuel.

The slant-4 was canted to the left by 45 degrees, which left the entire induction system perched atop the mill. It was mated to the Spitfire 4-speed gearbox and a rigid rear axle from the Dolomite sedans. The rear axle was controlled by two trailing arms, two radius rods, coil springs, and conventional shock absorbers. A stiff anti-roll bar was also fitted.

At the front were the industry-wide ubiquitous MacPherson struts with lower wishbones and anti-roll bar. The Adler & Alford rack-and-pinion steering used in many Triumph models was chosen and the entire assembly was attached to the car via a pressed-steel crossmember and rubber bushings.

The new car sat on 13-inch stamped steel wheels fitted with power-assisted 9-inch disc brakes at the front and 8-inch drum brakes at the rear.

Production of the Bullet concept began late in 1974 with the first cars being available in January of the following year.

TR7 unibodies coming down the line at the Speke production facility in Liverpool, England. Unfortunately, the factory, and the supply chain, were beset by labor issues including slowdowns and strikes. This resulted in gaps in production and quality issues in the initial production. The first cars were exported to the United States and it wasn't until 1976 that the rest of the world could take delivery. (Photo Courtesy Revs Institute/Karl Ludvigsen Collection)

The first cars were available in America only, which forced the rest of the world to wait until May 1976 to finally receive the TR7. In reality, labor issues and strikes at the Speke plant in Liverpool delayed the full startup of production and poor build quality plagued the TR7's introduction.

In the debut road test, *Road & Track*'s John Dinkel said that he found the steering heavy, slow, and dead-feeling but found the ride comfortable and the brakes worked well. Ultimately, he said this of the debut, "Even though it blazes no new trails in the evolution of the sports car, the TR-7 is a modern and refined car that will appeal to the buyer attracted to sports-car looks, handling, size, and character but turned off by a leaky windshield, buckboard rides, and ineffective heaters."

Styling is, of course, subjective, but from the moment the TR7 appeared, its looks caused a stir. Reviews of the car were filled with euphemisms including "odd," "eye-catching," "distinctive," and "exotic." Most journalists had trouble coming to terms with the large C-pillars and tall but stubby rear end on a relatively short 85-inch wheelbase (215.9 cm). Its low nose and coupe form also drew comparisons to the Fiat X1/9, Mazda RX-7, and Datsun 260Z, but the only advantage TR7 had over those cars was price. Mann's Bullet concept was considered to be forward, aggressive, and even risky at the time, but I believe that the design holds up well 40 years later.

Invoking hindsight again, is it reasonable to question whether or not this car should have been badged as a TR model? Should it have been called the Bullet? Was the TR a help or a hindrance? *Road & Track*'s John Lamm said in a road test that there is a link to its sports car ancestors.

The TR7 debuted at $5,100, which was about $1,000 more than the similarly wedged X1/9 or the MGB GT, but far less than the $7,000 Z-car. Unfortunately, it could not compete in the performance area. With just 92 horses available to lug the 2,250-pound car, it took 11.3 seconds to reach 60 mph and 18.5 seconds to cover the quarter-mile. At two-thirds of the cost, a Spitfire (granted, it's a very different type of car) could cover the same ground in 20 seconds and offer an open top. Despite the $2,000 premium, the silky smooth inline 6 of the Datsun made 150 hp, which was difficult to overlook. The TR series' more-bang-for-your-buck performance edge had been lost.

The press did agree on the restyled interior that had taken many cues from the American and Japanese cars. The characteristic wood and flat layout was replaced by up-to-date black vinyl and modern contours, which included well-labeled controls for a useful heater and windshield defogger. A pod housing all the new-look instruments was placed in front of the driver. As a sign of the times, the

The dashboard was a completely modern design with one modeled form stretching door to door. All the instruments were located in a binnacle behind the steering wheel. Once again, the display was dominated by a larger speedo and tach flanked on each side by two smaller dials. Fuel and charging (volts) gauges are on the right with temperature gauge and an analog clock on the left. Oil pressure was now monitored in a stack of warning lights in the center.

In the center of the cockpit, the molded dashboard flowed all the way to the transmission tunnel, giving it a fully integrated feel. Radio and climate controls were located ahead of the shifter and within easy reach of the driver or passenger. Aftermarket stereos were a common modification.

long-present oil pressure gauge was replaced by an analog clock. How's that for appealing to the American market?

All of the other no-nonsense controls were within easy reach of the driver. Heater and air conditioning levers flanked the stereo radio below the vents at the lower center of the console. Words such as heater and stereo were unheard of in previous TR models. As another sign-of-the-time design, wipers and lights were placed on steering column stalks. A large, padded black slab filled the center of the steering wheel to appease safety rules. However, the horn was activated by pushing on the turn-signal/headlight stalk. Other manufacturers did the same thing with the horn. It was silly and far from safe.

The TR7 also sported the widest cabin in TR history; the 66-inch wide (167.6 cm) body allowed for 61 roomy inches inside (154.9 cm). Large, reclining seats covered in a corduroy material made for an inviting interior.

The TR7 was the first TR in 10 years not to offer IRS or an overdrive transmission. The IRS was dead for good, but a form of overdrive was added in 1977 when the Rover 3500 5-speed gearbox and a beefier rear end were added to the lineup as standard equipment. This dropped final drive from 3.9 to 3.6 and revs dropped by 1,000 rpm for more comfortable highway cruising but yielded little in the way of fuel economy. An optional 3-speed Borg-Warner Type 65 automatic transmission was also offered in 1976, making it the first shiftless TR in Triumph history.

Appearance was changed with sportier alloy wheels with trim rings. The interior also received a freshening when the drop-head (convertible) version debuted in 1979. Color-coordinated plaid seat inserts with matching plaid trim on the door panels gave the cockpit a smart look. Interestingly, there were only two color options for this trim: navy blue and camel tan.

Because Triumph was given all the money to develop its new car it also launched an aggressive ad campaign trumpeting the styling of the new car. More than 15,000 TR7s were built during the first year and an all-time high of 25,820 cars were built in 1976 when the rest of the world finally got a crack at the car.

The non-U.S. version featured SU carburetors instead of the Strombergs on an easier-breathing engine that produced 105 hp and 119 ft-lbs of torque. The lack of safety bumpers gave it a trimmer 2,200-pound curb weight. This combination of weight and horsepower allowed it to reach 60 mph in 9.1 seconds and knocked 1.5 seconds off the quarter-mile time of its American cousin.

By 1977, the TR7 had hit its sales stride with more than 40,000 cars built in just two years. Plans were underway to boost performance and offer a convertible when Leyland was again beset with labor problems. Strikes, work stoppages, and sit-ins at the Speke assembly plant cost nearly an entire year of production. Just 5,500 1978 models were produced and all other plans were delayed or scrapped, including an up-rated engine. The labor situation proved to be untenable and eventually all Triumph production was moved to the Canley plant in 1978.

Overall build quality improved dramatically after assembly was in full swing in Canley. Canley-built cars are easily identified by the wreath on the nose panel.

CHAPTER 5: Seventh Heaven: Triumph Gets a Wedgie

One distinctive feature of the new car was the plaid cloth inserts in the seats and door panels, which gave a warm and luxurious feel to the car. Interiors were offered in navy blue or tan only, regardless of the exterior body color.

The base TR7 came with corduroy upholstery that the buyer could choose in either tan or black. The rest of the interior was trimmed in matching marbled vinyl. Long-legged drivers could not recline the seats because of the close proximity to the rear bulkhead. A small parcel shelf was situated just below the rear window. (Photo Courtesy Author Collection)

Finally, in 1979, the car and the company were re-introduced. The company was introduced as Jaguar Rover Triumph Inc. and the car was presented as the TR7 convertible. The coupe was still offered, but it was the convertible that caused the stir. The market had been pining for an open version since the debut of the new car.

With the notchy hardtop gone, the angular lines and steeply raked windshield of the new open version flowed nicely and transformed it from a GT car into a true sports car. At long last, the new car became the car everyone wanted.

Styling controversy was quickly forgotten as the press swooned over the new option. "The TR7 roadster is not for those who make a career out of being fun, but for those who like to have fun," said *Car and Driver*. *Road & Track* said, "The TR7 convertible must rank as one of the most comfortable, practical, and entertaining sports cars on the market today." And finally, *Motor Trend* said, "When it comes to drivability, the TR7 matches the Corvette in every respect."

It must be said that these new convertible tops worked very well. The operation was easy and they fit snuggly, keeping the elements out of the cockpit. It was a far cry from the removable bows, canvas, and snaps of days gone by. What was once a hindrance is now considered charming.

Mechanically, nothing was changed from the coupe with the exception of extra bracing to the subframe required to keep the car from becoming a flexible flyer. This put the weight at 2,450 pounds and sadly created even more of a drag on the already over-matched engine.

As exciting as the new roadster was to look at, the powerplant was incredibly unremarkable. EPA smog laws and the desire for fuel economy had choked the engine to just 85 hp. Coupling this engine with the 5-speed manual box was barely enough to keep the driver entertained during spirited driving. Then again, with those good looks and the sun shining, what more could a sports car lover need? More power is the obvious answer.

The true potential of the Bullet platform was on the verge of coming to fruition. British Leyland was, unfortunately, continuing to experience financial and production challenges. In 1980, the Canley plant was shuttered and all production was moved to the Rover plant in Solihull. Obviously, there is great cost in making a move like this. The upside was that just as Canley was an upgrade from Speke, Solihull was a step up from Canley. Quality continued to improve.

The real issue facing British Leyland was the exchange rate of the British Pound Sterling to the U.S. Dollar. The weakness of the pound to the dollar and the fact that the vast majority of cars were exported to the United States meant that Leyland was losing money on every car sold. Nevertheless, it soldiered on.

Plans were on the boards to replace the slant-4 in the TR7 with the most versatile and more reliable O-series engines. These were conventional carbureted 4-cylinder engines featuring a belt-driven overhead camshaft (OHC). The engine was better suited for the contemporary pollution control

TR7 convertibles coming down the line at the Solihull plant. The TR7 had three manufacturing homes through its life, beginning at the Speke plant, then moving to the Canley plant in 1978, with the final cars built at the Rover plant. Build quality improved with each move.

and the 94 hp output was scalable. Unfortunately, time ran out on the TR7 before it could receive the transplant.

Meanwhile, in 1977 several TR7 coupes were "pilot built" with the 3.5-liter Rover V-8. This was hardly groundbreaking since the original Bullet concept called for a V-8 in its earliest iterations. The Rover engine was clearly the most desirable engine for this application. True, Triumph already had its own SOHC V-8 in production in the Stag. That 3.0-liter was viewed as too large and too heavy for the new prototype. Unfortunately Rover had production all locked up. A few hundred TR8 test cars were built in 1978 and 1979 before the final TR8 was created. After years of speculation and pleading by the enthusiast press, the V-8–powered TR8 took its entrance bow in early 1980.

ONE OVER THE EIGHT

The lusty little 3.5-liter (215-ci) Rover aluminum V-8 dropped right into the existing space without even mentioning the word shoehorn. This fact alone validates the idea of V-8 power at the time it was originally designed. The exception was that the battery was relocated to the trunk in an effort to save space as much as it was to counterbalance the heavier front end. Stiffer springs all around were also necessary.

The compact, all-aluminum V-8 was a derivative of the Oldsmobile and Buick designs from the early 1960s. It began as the Buick 215-ci engine that debuted in 1960. At just 318 pounds, comparable to many cast-iron 4-cylinders, the alloy mill pumped out 200 hp; it was relatively easy to coax more power from it. Oldsmobile offered a turbocharged version with a variation in the cylinder head to create more power. A small number of Pontiacs also received the mighty little mill.

Unfortunately, it suffered from oil leaks and cooling issues; it was pulled from production in 1963. Rover saw the merits of the diminutive V-8 for its cars and in 1965 bought the tooling from General Motors. Rover used steel cylinder liners to help cure some of the ills. It also used a redesigned intake manifold aspirated by dual SU carburetors. These changes increased the weight of the ex-Buick V-8 by 57 pounds but resulted in a stronger, more reliable engine.

Of course, what would a late-model TR be without some influence from the EPA? Two versions were required in the United States to comply with the laws: one for California and one for the rest of the country.

The "regular" version was fed by dual Stromberg carbs while the West Coast received a fuel-injected version. The former was rated at 133 hp at 5,000 rpm and 174 ft-lbs of torque while the latter made 137 hp at 168 ft-lbs of torque.

In the debut road test, Road & Track reported no appreciable difference in a head-to-head test of fuel injection and the dual-carb setup. The carbureted V-8's 0-60–time was clocked at 8.4 seconds, trimming a full 3.1 seconds off the TR7's 4-cylinder–powered time.

The new model fell down in two areas: braking and fuel consumption. Brakes are obviously the most noteworthy

At long last an 8-cylinder version of the Wedge was announced for 1978. The TR8 featured the same handsome good looks, wind in the hair, and kick-in-the-pants performance that were hallmarks of the first TRs.

CHAPTER 5: Seventh Heaven: Triumph Gets a Wedgie

Outwardly there was little to distinguish the TR7 roadster from the new TR8 except for some badging and larger tires.

Finally, in 1979, a roadster version of the TR7 was offered. The rakish lines of the body worked well with the top down, as if it should have always been a convertible.

knock here. The power-assisted disc/drum setup had very long stopping distances (180 feet from 60 mph) and was prone to lock-up. The 9.8-inch discs up front with 9.0-inch drums at the rear could have been beefier. Then again, consider the American cars that came from Detroit with burly 400-ci V-8s that were stopped with a single-pot master cylinder and 4-wheel drum brakes. Granted, that was 10 years earlier.

The claimed EPA figures of 22 mpg were proved to actually deliver a figure in the mid-teens. But when it comes to sports cars, is this a question any owner really asks?

Ultimately, *Road & Track* said this about its first drive in the TR8: "The TR8 doubles as a pussycat around town and a tiger on the open road."

At just $12,000 it was a high-powered bargain, beating the likes of Mazda RX-7, Datsun 280ZX, and Porsche 924 by $8,000. But the most arresting figure was the torque, which beat any of its contemporaries by as much as 80 percent. The fuel-injected version could reach 60 mph in 8.1 seconds and cover the quarter-mile in 16.2, which also compared favorably. Brakes, wheels, and tires remained the same as the TR7, which hurt it under braking and on the skid pad.

Outwardly, there was little to distinguish the robusto version from its slightly underpowered predecessor. The square center bulge in the hood became a little larger, there were dual exhaust pipes, and some understated decals. Cosmetically, everything remained the same inside and out. The TR8 received the sportier and more attractive Moto Lita padded steering wheel.

Alas, it's once again the "what could have been" scenario for the TR8 and for Triumph. After five years of development, controversy, and production strife, the Bullet finally achieved its potential of sexy good looks and world-class performance. It was certainly on par with any of its contemporaries from Europe and Japan. And delivering it in a value-priced package.

Just as the TR8 went into production, development work was being done on a new TR7 with different engines, and even an MG-badged variant, the company fell on more hard times. Cash was tight and as factories were consolidated, several models were canceled, including the Spitfire and MGB. The all-important U.S. market had fallen into a recession and the disparity between the dollar and the pound would have put the TR8's price over $20,000.

The SOHC 3.5-liter Rover V-8 transformed the pleasant sports tourer to a bona fide performance sports car. The engine lineage comes from the Buick/Oldsmobile 215-ci aluminum mill; Rover purchased the rights to it in the 1960s. It weighed no more than the 4-cylinder it was replacing but delivered 60 percent more power. Of course, it's difficult to actually see the engine because it was shoehorned into the tight space. In addition, the significant amount of pollution control hoses hide any hint of any engine.

The TR8 was canceled in 1980 with the last cars produced in 1981. Because of the labor issues and production changes, specific production figures are not known, but a variety of reports suggest around 2,700 TR8s were produced with almost all of them for the U.S. market. Only 35 TR8s were built with right-hand drive. By mid-1981 British Leyland was out of the sports car business for good.

So did Leyland achieve its goal with the Bullet project? Although the TR7 was a totally new look, the company still ended up raiding parts bins, making compromises, and delivering a hard-topped coupe that did not offer a real price or performance advantage. Some argue if the car should have been in the TR family at all. But if you wish to make that argument then you must define what a sports car is, especially by 1970s standards.

The TR8 finally made good on all the promises of the new platform. Unfortunately, it was too late and there was no saving it.

A common and fairly simple modification for all V-8 owners is to change the intake system. Here, the dual-SU carbs have been replaced with a Holley 4-barrel and aluminum manifold. The owner reports greatly improved throttle response and power. Stripping away the carburetors, air boxes, and numerous hoses reveals the engine. Obviously, this example also sports Offenhauser valvecovers.

Life inside the TR8 was very civilized. Plush carpets lined the footwells and there was ample padding and comfort throughout. The functional dashboard remained unchanged throughout the run and the tartan accents also remained.

Triumph continued to battle the scrutiny of U.S. emissions lawmakers. California was the most draconian, so the V-8 was mated with a Bosch L-Jetronic fuel-injection system to meet the West Coast code. The injection version was rated nearer to 140 hp. Only a few hundred were produced before production shut down for good.

The TR7 and TR8 cockpit was by far the most comfortable of any car in the TR family. It was fully carpeted, padded, and trimmed out from top to bottom. It was also the first car in the line to include the U.S.-mandated crash beams in the doors. The wedge shape gave the car a low center of gravity and, thus, reasonably good handling.

CHAPTER 5: Seventh Heaven: Triumph Gets a Wedgie

THE STAG: TRIUMPH'S OTHER V-8

Triumph never really planned to offer a Gran Tourismo–type of sports touring car. The Stag came about as a happenstance styling exercise derived from the development of the 2000 sedan. And once again it was Giovanni Michelotti's pen that spawned an exciting car for the times.

In 1966, Michelotti and Harry Webster were putting the finishing touches on the new line of sedans when Michelotti asked if he could create a sports version to use at motor shows and other expos to promote his design studio. The only caveat was that if Triumph liked his concepts they would have first refusal on the design. As it turned out, Webster liked the car so much that he brought the prototype back to Coventry before anyone else saw it.

The code name Stag was a hit in the executive offices and was green-lighted. It was initially to be powered by the 2.5-liter inline 6-cylinder with fuel injection, but Webster saw it as an opportunity for the newly developed 2.5-liter OHC V-8. This Triumph-built engine was decidedly different from the 3.0-liter Rover (ex-Buick) design. Outwardly, it looked like two 4-cylinders married together by a common block. (It's interesting to note that it was essentially half of this engine that was used in the initial TR7.)

Unfortunately, Stag was mired in Triumph's never-ending budget and production problems. Nevertheless, Webster kept the concept alive and, finally, in 1970, the Stag was introduced to the market as a "new kind of Triumph."

The original 1966 styling was freshened to match the rest of the line. It was fitted with the house-made V-8 that had now evolved to a full 3.0 liters (2,997 cc). The intended fuel injection system could not deliver acceptable anti-smog numbers so dual Zenith-Stromberg 175CD carbs were used to make 145

The 1300 was British Leyland's first front-wheel-drive car. Designed by Michelotti, it was to be the successor to the Herald. It featured the same 1,296-cc powerplant mounted transversely. Perhaps this was not one of his best designs, but he worked with the materials he was given. The difficulty was that the engine sat atop the transmission, making the entire assembly very tall. This necessitated the grille and front clip to be taller than it might have been ordinarily. (Photo Courtesy Moss Motors)

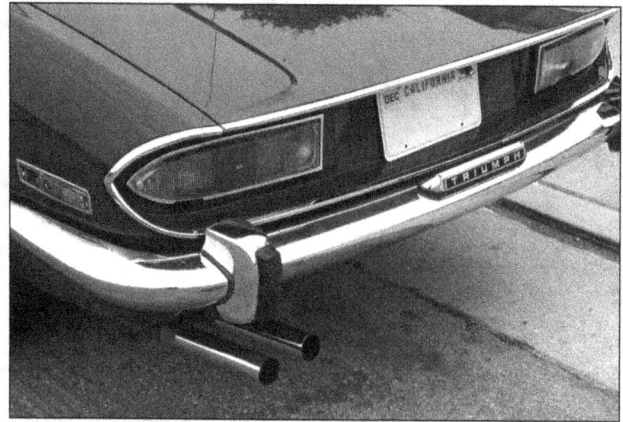

The rear view of the 1300 was slightly unusual, namely the additional overhang on the roofline above the rear window. Most important, the rear styling of the 1300 gave way to the rear-end treatment on nearly all Triumphs from the sedan's debut in 1965 through the 1970s. In fact, a number of cars, such as the GT6 Mark 3 for example, were restyled to match this look. (Photo Courtesy Moss Motors)

Unlike the 1300, Michelotti's design for the Stag was spot-on for what the car was envisioned to be: an upmarket four-seat sports car. Introduced as a "new kind of Triumph," it was a mid-size, open British car with Italian flair. The Stag came into being at the behest of Harry Webster, who asked Michelotti to design a sports derivative of the Triumph 2000 that he was working on in the mid-1960s. The car was well received and Triumph had high hopes for it. A Stag even made a cameo in the 1971 James Bond movie *Diamonds Are Forever*. (Photo Courtesy Moss Motors)

hp. Fuel economy was rated at 17 mpg and 0–60 mph was clocked at 11.5 seconds.

The unibody design rode on MacPerson struts and coil springs at the front with the IRS coming from the 2000 sedan. Driver's directives were transmitted via rack-and-pinion steering.

The drophead coupe boasted a true 2+2 seating configuration with such luxury features as wood-veneer dash fascia with a full cluster of gauges, power windows, and optional Borg-Warner 3-speed automatic transmission. The 4-speed was, of course, standard.

As development continued, the U.S. government was still sending mixed signals regarding the future of convertible tops. This gave way to one of the Stag's most distinctive features. Beneath the convertible top, a T-bar provided roll-over protection. These roof beams remained in place whether in convertible trim or with the optional removable hardtop. In addition to the safety benefits, the design offered greater body strength and rigidity. In some ways it could be considered a precursor to the T-tops that became popular in the mid-1970s. Unfortunately, the window frames also remained in place and detracted from the look a bit.

The nicely appointed Stag debuted at $5,600 (£1,600) in mid-1970. Considering a comparably equipped E-Type cost upward of $7,000, it was a value. Sadly, it failed to find its niche. Performance was deemed merely adequate and the early cars were plagued with fit and finish issues, faulty electrics, and leaky head gaskets. The Stag was pulled from the U.S. market in 1973 but carried on in Britain through 1977. More than 25,000 Stags were built, but fewer than 4,000 made it to the United States.

The Stag's most distinctive feature was a T-bar structure that connected the windshield to a rollbar of sorts mounted where a B-pillar would be. The design provided roll-over protection while also giving structural rigidity to the unibody. The T-bar was permanently mounted with the convertible top or optional hardtop, which was raised over the bar. (Photo Courtesy Moss Motors)

The Stag featured the new Triumph OHC V-8 when it was launched in 1970. It was initially planned for fuel to be delivered by a mechanical fuel-injection system. As was the case with so many fuel systems, the fuel-injection unit was unable to comply with U.S. pollution-control regulations. Dual Zenith-Stromberg 175CD carbs were used to make 145-hp. (Photo Courtesy Moss Motors)

Life inside the Stag was very comfortable. A sporting steering wheel and full complement of gauges greeted the driver. The 4-speed shift lever, or optional automatic shift handle, felt easily at hand. It even had power windows. Front seats were quite comfortable; however, the rear seats might only be good for small children or adults out for a very short trip. (Photo Courtesy Moss Motors)

CHAPTER 6
THE BOMB GOES OFF

Triumph's secret project, code name Bomb, was introduced as the Spitfire 4 at the London Motor Show in Earls Court in October 1962. Today, the car is known as the Mark 1 because its successor was called the Mark 2 and the script number "4" disappeared from the trunk lid.

The Spitfire Mark 1 debuted at the London Motor Show at Earls Court in October 1962. The car that was unveiled to the public had been rushed to market in just 14 months. In truth it was only the final phase of styling that was rushed. An actual finished car had existed for more than two years prior to the launch.

Alick Dick and his team began talking of a new series of small cars, code named Zobo, in late 1956 as the TR3 was gathering steam around the world. Unfortunately, Triumph was not able to move ahead with the new concept because it once again lacked two very important elements to producing the new concept: styling and body manufacturing.

The initial concept was for a unibody design. However, Triumph had always contracted-out all body construction and therefore had no means to produce large quantities of unibodies internally. This problem was further exacerbated when Triumph's rival BMC acquired Fisher & Ludlow, the shop that Triumph relied on most heavily for bodywork.

Furthermore, no one in-house could agree on styling for the new small cars.

Alick Dick was left with no choice but to abandon the unibody concept and return to the separate frame and chassis configuration for the new small cars. This technique was not considered cutting edge, but it did allow for unique bodies to be placed on the same running gear across different models. In this case, the new Herald platform was used. When looking at the two cars side-by-side, it does seem a bit incongruous that the boxy Herald shared the same general chassis as the sporting new two-seater. They had agreed on the platform but needed a body design for a pure two-seat sports car.

Once again, Giovanni Michelotti saved the day. Michelotti was given the Zobo project, which was to come up with successors to the Standard 8 and Standard 10 sedans. Again, the original goal was a unibody car, but they had to settle for a traditional frame with the body bolted to the top. Michelotti quickly penned several designs for two-door coupes with hints of the razor-edge styling. In 1959, the Triumph Herald debuted.

The Herald chassis featured fully independent suspension through a coil spring over a shock absorber/wishbone setup at the front and a transverse leaf spring/swing axle setup at the rear. The rack-and-pinion steering, coupled with the front suspension, produced an incredibly tight turning circle; the wheels could aim almost perpendicular to the direction of the car. This car was the foundation of the Spitfire.

While Michelotti was working on the sedan design, Alick Dick gave him the task of designing the Zobo sports car derivative, code named Bomb. Although not exactly a secret assignment, it wasn't widely known that Michelotti was working on it.

Unfortunately, the sports car took a back burner to the family car as Triumph continued to struggle to stay afloat. Some 14 new models (including TR3A, TR3B, and TR4) were introduced between the beginning of project Bomb in 1957 and its eventual debut in 1962. Tooling and time gobbled up resources that would have gone into the new car.

Triumph's competitors simultaneously introduced a number of small sports cars that received positive reviews and brisk sales. This included the Austin-Healey "Frogeye" Sprite ("Bugeye" in the United States), MG Midget, Alfa Romeo Giulietta Spider, and Fiat 1200. The Sprite and the market's reception attracted Triumph's attention and project Bomb was accelerated.

In late 1960, Michelotti's first prototype was delivered to Coventry from his Turin facility. The timing of the arrival was unlucky; it coincided with Standard-Triumph's financial well once again running dry. The newly launched Herald was being lambasted in the press for poor workmanship, and sales were slow. Domestic (U.K.) sales of the TRs and Vanguards were virtually nonexistent (a paltry 63 TR3As sold in 1961). Needless to say, money was tight. It was around this time that Alick Dick, the project's biggest champion, left the company. So the new prototype was covered, placed in a corner, and left for dead.

Late in the summer of 1961, shortly after Leyland Motors' takeover of Triumph, the new managing director, Stanley Markland, was touring the Coventry plant. He spied the dusty prototype in the corner and after one look at the car he approved the project on the spot and ordered it to be ready for the London Motor Show the following October.

The final production model differed very little from Michelotti's original concept. The first prototype was delivered to the Canley plant in Coventry in 1960, but Triumph had other sales and production concerns at the time. It was parked in a corner, covered, and left there. While touring the plant in 1961, Leyland's managing director spotted the car and, upon sight, ordered it into production.

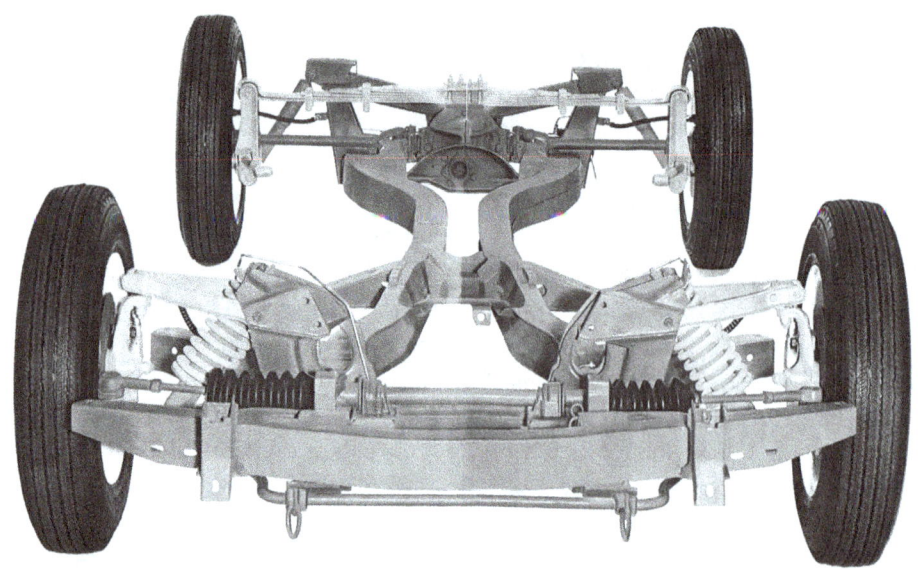

The new small sports car was based on the Herald sedan (also designed by Michelotti) and shared many chassis and trim components. This sales brochure illustrates the unique "backbone" frame to which the body was bolted. Rack-and-pinion steering can be seen at the front with coil and wishbone suspension. The most remarkable characteristic was the ability to turn the front wheels nearly perpendicular to the direction of travel, which resulted in a turning circle of just 24 feet. (Photo Courtesy Author Collection)

The notoriously flexible Herald frame was replaced with a backbone-type chassis/frame with a wheelbase of 6 feet 11 inches. This is 8½ inches shorter than the Herald's 7-foot 7-inch wheelbase. This backbone arrangement required the body shell to have reinforced sills to replace the outer frame rails and a beefed-up rear end for the suspension mounting points.

The new car was given the same front suspension and steering layout as its ancestor with coil spring over shock absorber and wishbones in front and the transverse leaf spring with high-pivot swing axle at the rear. The-rack-and pinion steering delivered the same remarkable 24-foot turning circle. Barely two full turns of the steering wheel and the front wheels were almost perpendicular to the direction of the car. It wore 9-inch disc brakes at the front with 7-inch drums at the rear; 13-inch steel wheels were standard.

In the United States, Chevrolet's Corvette was gathering a great deal of press. Subsequently, the notion arose of crafting this new sports car out of fiberglass. Closer to home, Daimler had just introduced the SP250 Dart that featured a fiberglass body. However, with no resources and no time, a stamped steel body was the only way to go.

The body was a unique one-piece design to provide the necessary strength and support. With a nod to the Herald design, the front fenders and hood was a one-piece unit that pivoted at the front to allow incredible access to the engine bay. Pulling a styling cue from its bigger sibling's trim features, a thin chrome bead ran the length of the front and rear fenders. To keep the hood line as low as

The Spitfire 4 script is clearly visible on the trunk lid. The 4 was rarely referred to in advertising and subsequently dropped with the next incarnation. Also visible are the chrome fender beads on the tops of the fenders. They were simply a body accent that harkened back to the functional beading on the TR3.

It wasn't as simple as merely grafting the newly minted body onto the existing Herald frame. While the Spitfire owes its heritage to the Herald and shares a number of common parts, the chassis is very much removed from the Herald platform.

possible, a short radiator was used with the tank mounted longitudinally alongside the cylinder head. It was a unique solution to the space issue and it worked surprisingly well. There was enough space and air under the hood to prevent the tank from becoming too hot.

The diminutive and austere first-generation Austin-Healey Sprite in an original period photo. The Mark 1 version was designed to be simple and affordable, offering only the most basic elements. No trunk, side curtains rather than windows, and a very spartan cockpit. Healey's 948-cc engine produced 43 hp and a 0-60–mph time over 20 seconds. The first Spitfire 4 offered greater comfort and performance from day one. (Photo Courtesy British Motor Industry Heritage Trust)

The 39-hp 1,147-cc Herald engine was modified to produce 63 hp at 5,750 rpm. Modifications came in the form of twin 1¼-inch SU carburetors, increasing compression to 9:1, and a slightly hotter cam. These changes gave the new car a 0-60–mph time of 15 seconds, a top speed of 90 mph, and still producing a respectable 30 mpg. The Spitfire also used Herald's 4:11.1 rear end and 4-speed gearbox. No overdrive was initially offered on the car. The mesh grille inserts were shared with the Herald and, of course, all electrics were Lucas from the Triumph store of parts. The next order of business was to beat the spartan Sprites and Midgets at their own game.

Doors on the prototype were made deeper to allow for roll-up windows. Front disc brakes were standard as was a locking trunk. Even windshield washers were standard. The Spitfire also had ample interior space, unlike the shoulder-to-shoulder seating in the Healey and MG. It was initially thought that the 63 bhp would be enough to suck the Frogeye headlights out of the little 43-hp Healey, but just as the Spitfire came to market the diminutive 948-cc Sprite engine was upgraded to 1,098 cc. Nevertheless, at £730 ($2,199) the new car was just £62 more than a Sprite and £70 less than elder sibling TR4.

There are no records to indicate how the car's code name of Bomb became Spitfire. In fact, when the wraps initially came off the new car, it was actually named Spitfire 4. In time, the name Spitfire created endless advertising opportunities linking it to the famous British fighter plane of World War II. Nevertheless, the Spitfire marked Michelotti's finest hour at Triumph. His TR4 was handsome and stylish in a brutish way while the Herald was nothing short of boxy. The Spitfire was sleek, smooth, and flowed from nose to tail because Michelotti was given the freedom to create this car in its entirety.

Carried over from the Herald was the 1,147-cc engine. Horsepower was pushed to 63 through the addition of twin 1¼-inch SU carburetors and increasing the compression to 9:1. Top speed was rated at 90 mph while still delivering an economical 30 mpg.

The twin SU carburetors mounted on the horizontal manifold. The 0-60–mph time was clocked at a very adequate 15.5 seconds. Although this would not be classified as neck-snapping power, the small size and open cockpit made it exhilarating to row through the gears.

CHAPTER 6: The Bomb Goes Off

The unique one-piece body was strengthened to bolt to the minimal frame. Similar to the large one-piece hood on its cousin Herald, the Spitfire also had a large one-piece unit that tilted forward for incomparable access to the power unit.

Mark 1 Spitfire bodies waiting to be mated with their chassis. The Herald sedan chassis was shortened by 8½ inches to become the underpinnings of the Spitfire. The Herald's strengthening outer side rails were removed, which meant that the body tub required reinforcement to provide the required rigidity. (Photo Courtesy British Motor Industry Heritage Trust)

While the Spitfire edged the Sprite in standard equipment, the interior was not exactly filled with plushness and luxury. Molded rubber mats replaced carpets and things such as the dashboard-bracing ribs were clearly visible as they arched over the tall tunnel just ahead of the gear lever. Octagonal mounting bolts were in plain sight. The Smiths speedometer, tachometer, temperature, and fuel gauges were placed in the middle of the dash in a black crinkle-finish surround. The center mount for the instruments made it simple (and cheap) to swap from right-hand to left-hand steering for export. Wipers, lights, and optional heater were controlled by knobs beneath the instruments and large parcel shelves below each side of the dash finished the symmetry of the layout.

The windshield was shared with the TR4 and was initially planned to be detachable in keeping with Triumph's sporting image. The removable windshield was not carried over to the final production version in favor of greater rigidity and weather repellency.

The removable bows for the top stowed neatly in the trunk with the vertical elements tucking forward beneath the fenders. The inside of the trunk was unfinished, body seams were exposed, and a scissor jack mounted overtly on the left-side fender arch. A vinyl cover separated the spare tire from the small luggage space.

At Earls Court, the Spitfire 4 was an instant hit. The enthusiast press practically tripped over themselves in praising the car. "This is a fast sports car that has perfect town manners and an appearance that will break down the sales resistance of many prospective owners," said *Autosport*. *Modern Motor* said, "You get so much more for your money than with any other low-priced sports car."

The lightweight car was certainly exhilarating to drive. Criticisms of it came in the form of backhanded compliments about the rear suspension. Indeed it was an inexpensive and genius way to allow Triumph to boast about IRS in its new small sports car. The swing-axle design was unique among the liter-class sports cars and Spitfire's short wheel travel gave it some distinct characteristics.

The stiffer springs produced a hard ride on rough roads and the rear could even "hop" when hitting bumps at high speed. The staccato bouncing reverberated through the entire car. In low-speed corners, the rear wheels tended toward negative camber and induced mild understeer.

A row of early Spitfire 4s receiving a coat of Signal Red paint at the Canley factory in 1963. Red cars received a black interior, although some of the very earliest versions were trimmed with red upholstery. It's reported that 45,753 of the first generation of Spitfires rolled out of Canley. (Photo Courtesy British Motor Industry Heritage Trust)

The Spitfire's chief competition was Austin-Healey's Sprite. The cockpit trumped the more spartan Sprite by featuring full door panels, roll-up windows, and more contoured seatbacks with better upholstery.

However, in fast-cornering situations the rear wheels took on some alarming camber angles and triggered pronounced oversteer. In extremely tight corners the inside rear wheel actual lifted enough for the tire to completely lose contact with the road surface. After it straightened out, the driver was alerted to the tire returning to contact with the road by the audible squealing.

The press repeatedly used words such as "safe" and "controllable" when describing this phenomenon, but it was Car and Driver that was the most prophetic about the potential of the car when it said, "Spitfire has a good chance to take over the position as Triumph's best-selling car in the U.S. market."

The clandestine Bomb project was an instant hit and orders poured in. Unfortunately, Forward Radiator, which was building the body shells, had only established temporary tooling because it expected the new car to sell in far fewer numbers, similar to the TR4. A total of 1,355 Spitfires were built in 1962. By January 1963, Triumph was producing more than 1,250 cars per month; it shipped 20,950 by year's end.

Triumph was able to maintain the more-for-your-money edge over Sprite and Midget by adding three options late in 1963 that improved drivability and enhanced appearance. A smart-looking steel hardtop transformed the car into a weather-tight coupe and a Laycock overdrive for third and fourth gears made long trips and highway driving more bearable. Center-mount 48-spoke 4½-inch-wide wire wheels could be ordered, which further increased the Spitfire's sporting charm. A total of 45,753 Spitfires were built between October 1962 and April 1965.

MARK 2

Spitfire sales remained brisk and BMC was forced to up the ante. In 1964, a new Sprite and Midget, now boasting roll-up windows among other minor improvements, were introduced. But Triumph countered with the introduction of the Spitfire Mark 2 in March 1965.

Differences between the original and the Mark 2 were subtle but enough to call it a new model in the face of competition. Carpets replaced the rubber mats in the footwells and most of the painted metal surfaces in the cockpit were now covered with vinyl trim panels. The seats were improved for more comfort. The grille had only horizontal

Around the time that the Spitfire was in development, there was a proliferation of fiberglass-bodied sports cars being built around the world. The success of the Corvette in the United States is well documented. Daimler had introduced its fiberglass-bodied SP250 Dart in 1959. The ladder frame coupled with the fiberglass body flexed so much that the doors opened on their own. Chrysler forced Daimler to drop the Dart name. It was the last new model introduced by Daimler before being acquired by Jaguar. (Photo Courtesy John Allan)

Gauges and controls were centered in the symmetrical dashboard. Four simple Jaeger gauges told the driver speed, revs, temperature, and remaining fuel. Basic control knobs lined up below the cluster. The center-mounted controls coupled with the simple symmetry of the dash made it easy for the factory to swap between right- and left-hand drive. This owner added supplemental oil pressure and vacuum gauges.

The chronology of the Spitfire is filled with small tweaks rather than wholesales changes. The Mark 2 featured small cosmetic changes, most notably horizontal bars that replaced the mesh squares in the grille opening. This example has also been modified with knock-on wire wheels.

Another illustration of the exemplary access to the mechanicals of the Mark 2. The 1,147-cc engine was retooled to produce 67 hp. The green color shown here was not standard but makes for a stunning presentation.

The rear of the Mark 2 was unchanged except for the Mark 2 script on the trunk lid. The number "4" designation used on the introductory model was seldom referenced and quietly phased out with the new model. The idea of a 6-cylinder version would have to wait a few more years.

The Mark 2 with the contrasting three-window folding top in place. Putting up the top was not difficult but it could be a bit fiddly. The top bows were stored in the trunk and the separate top had to be stretched over the frame. Some finger strength was required to get the entire perimeter snapped into place.

A removable hardtop was available on the Spitfire from its inception. Two bolts on the windshield header and a few more at the back of the cockpit and the car was airtight, although slightly claustrophobic. Here, a young couple illustrates the ease of installation. (Photo Courtesy British Motor Industry Heritage Trust)

bars instead of mesh and "Mark 2" appeared in script on the trunk lid, replacing the old "Spitfire 4."

As mentioned previously, the car was originally introduced as the Spitfire 4 and featured an elegant chrome script on the right trunk lid. However, throughout its first three years on the market, the "4" was almost completely ignored and never referenced. It did appear in early advertising, but it was never acknowledged and its meaning was never explained, not in articles and not even by the factory. It was quietly removed in favor of the Mark 2 badge in 1965 models.

Triumph retooled the manifolds of the 1,147-cc engine, coaxing 4 more horsepower; it now boasted 67 hp at 6,000 rpm. The Bellville spring washer clutch assembly was replaced with a 6½-inch diaphragm unit. The price of the Mark 2 had increased to £800 ($2,250), but it remained the best bang-for-your-buck sports car on the market.

The Spitfire was something of a cash cow for Triumph because it was fairly inexpensive to produce and was selling very well. Production carried on without any noteworthy changes.

MARK 3

Two years and 37,400 units later, the Mark 3 was introduced. BMC had again tipped the scales in its favor with the announcement of the Sprite Mark IV and Midget III in 1966. The new cars, dubbed Spridgets because of their interchangeability, now featured a 1.3-liter, 65-hp engine at just $2,130. Triumph immediately responded with a better, faster car.

Bore was increased by 4.4 mm on the 1,147-cc engine to deliver a final capacity of 1,296 cc. A new cylinder head based on the successful eight-port design used in the Le Mans campaign was fitted. The original 1¼-inch SU carburetors were retained to deliver a final output of 75 hp at 6,000 rpm with a top speed of 100 mph.

Larger Girling front calipers were added for better brake performance and the electrical system was switched to a negative ground to make it more user-friendly in the United States, where most of the cars were sold.

Cosmetically, the wraparound front bumper was raised a few inches to meet U.S. safety specifications. The radiator opening was narrowed and made open across the width of the car, which gave the Mark 3 something of a shark-nose look.

In the cockpit, drivers were greeted with the three-spoke "banjo" steering wheel inherited from the TR4. Wood-veneer trim now surrounded the center instrument cluster and a permanently attached folding top with zip-out rear window replaced the detachable top from its predecessor. Reverse lights were added to the rear panel below the trunk lid seam and seatbelt mountings were now standard. Later in the Mark 3's run, radial tires became standard equipment and were mounted on 4½-inch-wide rims.

CHAPTER 6: The Bomb Goes Off

The Spitfire received a light cosmetic makeover for 1967 with a new front-end and bumper treatment. Ride height was raised to meet U.S. safety requirements and a full wraparound front bumper was fitted, which gave the car a bit of a shark-nose appearance. (Photo Courtesy Author Collection)

The new front end gave the Mark 3 a more modern, integrated appearance. The forward-tipping hood was modified to accommodate the changes and the impact requirements. Under the hood, bore was increased on the 1,147-cc to 1,296 cc delivering 75 hp. (Photo Courtesy Manuel Pisani)

The rear of the Mark 3 was trimmed with neater bumpers and reverse lights were added for safety. The instrument cluster was still in the middle but it now featured a wood surround. The top assembly that was previously stowed in the trunk was replaced with a permanently mounted apparatus. In 1969, the instrument panel was redesigned in the theme of the TRs with speedo and tach in front of the steering wheel. Fuel and oil pressure were in the center of the black dashboard. (Photo Courtesy Manuel Pisani)

Midway through the Mark 3 in 1968, the 100,000th Spitfire rolled off the assembly line in Canley. Nearly 50 percent of all Spitfires were shipped to the United States with another 25 percent exported to Europe. (Photo Courtesy Manuel Pisani)

At $2,285, the Spitfire was still a bargain and offered more performance and more space than the Sprite at $2,130. It was also substantially less expensive than the Datsun 1600 at $2,766. Demand for the new model soared and 65,320 cars were built between 1967 and the fall of 1970. In fact, the Spitfire hit 100,000 units built in late 1967.

Everything was going well for the Spitfire. However, during the early life of the Mark 3, major outside forces were coming to bear that affected the future of the car. In the United States, where most of the cars were sold, attention to emissions and crashworthiness was heightened and legislators were coming down hard. The latter would not have such a big impact on the styling of the Spitfire, at least not for the time being. However, the new anti-smog laws were literally choking the performance out of the car.

By 1970, U.S. clean-air legislation had required Triumph to drop the dual SUs and fit a single Zenith-Stromberg carburetor to pass emissions standards. Horsepower dropped to 68 bhp. It was a new car with essentially the same performance as its five-year-old predecessor. Of course, the United States was the only country with these concerns. Throughout the rest of the world, Spitfire buyers were enjoying the same old performance.

Meanwhile, back at home Leyland Motors bought Rover in 1967. In 1968, it acquired British Motor Holdings, which included Jaguar, Austin-Healey, and MG. The arch rivals were suddenly part of the same family and the future of the Spitfire, and its rivals, was unclear.

MARK IV

Michelotti and the Triumph design team began work on the all-new Spitfire in 1968; it debuted as the Mark IV in October 1970. Although it looks like a simple update of the Mark 3, it is, in fact, a completely new car with all new

The new Mark IV cockpit was upgraded with a full-width dashboard that moved the main dials from the center to in front of the driver. Seats and door panels were also upgraded and coupled with the full-width carpets. The new interior made it feel more like a deluxe sports car. (Photo Courtesy George Krause)

panels. As with many previous design changes at Triumph, it was mostly new.

Part of the requirements for the new design was that the center section and doors were to be retained. Michelotti was free to tailor the nose and tail with a more contemporary look so he went back to a concept he had floated in 1965. It became another "what could have been" moment in Triumph's history.

Years earlier, Michelotti had designed a successor to the Mark 3 that was dubbed Fury. It was a unibody, or monocoque, design with the Triumph 2000 sedan as the base donor. The most prominent features of the sporty two-seater were the 6-cylinder 90-hp engine and pop-up headlights. It was a handsome design that truly looked like the next evolution in the Spitfire line. It was ahead of its time and could have catapulted Spitfire to new heights in performance and sales. At

As early as 1968, Triumph and Michelotti began working on code name Fury. It was to be a completely new Spitfire using modern unibody construction and powered by the 90-hp inline 6-cylinder from the 2000 sedan. Michelotti's gorgeous prototype was shelved because of the cost of tooling for the monocoque body and fear that the U.S. market would outlaw retractable headlamps. (Photo Courtesy Mike Garland)

The car grew in length by 4 inches and the faux fender beading was dropped; all surface panels were made smoother and sleeker. The flat trunk lid and vertical rear panel gave more luggage space and the redesign helped tie the Spitfire stylistically to the rest of the Triumph lineup. (Photo Courtesy George Krause)

The stroked version of the 1,296-cc engine was used to counter the ever-tightening emissions laws in the United States. Outwardly, it looked no different from its predecessor. The U.S. models used a single Zenith-Stromberg carburetor that produced 57 hp while the rest of the world retained the dual carbs that made 71 hp. *Road & Track*'s editor-in-chief Thomas Bryant proclaimed that the Spitfire was "still a kick to drive." (Photo Courtesy Andy Robinson)

the same time Toyota unveiled the amazing 2000GT at the Tokyo Motor Show. The sleek coupe with retractable headlights and 6-cylinder power catapulted Toyota onto the international stage. Fury could have done the same for Triumph.

Unfortunately, the unibody was dismissed out of hand for cost and the pop-up headlights were vetoed because of fear that U.S. legislators were about to outlaw the feature. About the only thing that Michelotti was able to salvage from his inspired design was the flat tail treatment that was already being used on other Triumph models such as the Stag.

The new Mark IV grew in overall length by 4 inches. The rear was lengthened and given a flat trunk lid that provided more luggage space. The flat rear panel treatment with integrated taillights was derived from the Stag, although it had become prevalent on other Triumph cars.

The center crown in the hood was eliminated with a smoother, tapered design that dropped at the nose to meet the new front bumper regulations. Two oversize chunks of shock-absorbing rubber flanked the grille opening below the front bumper. At the rear, a one-piece full-width bumper replaced the two chrome corner bumpers.

The 1500 was the final step in the evolution of Spitfire powerplants. The larger-displacement engines were needed to combat the restrictive U.S. emissions regulations and were rushed into production in 1973. The rest of the world did not receive the new model until 1975. U.S.-spec models were further handicapped by having a single Zenith-Stromberg carburetor rather than the dual SUs used in European versions. (Photo Courtesy Andy Robinson)

The Spitfire 1500 was introduced to the market in 1975, although the 1,493-cc powerplant had been installed in all U.S.-destined cars since 1973. All production models received the 1500 from 1975 onward. The 1500 models are easily identified by large rubber overrriders below the chrome bumpers. The 1500 decals on the hood and trunk only lasted for the first two model years. (Photo Courtesy Andy Robinson)

Inside, the cockpit was made more cozy and luxurious. The most noticeable change was the full-width wood-veneer dashboard. The speedo and tach were relocated in front of the driver behind the new alloy, three-spoke steering wheel. Fuel and temperature gauges remained in the center section just below the heater and vent controls.

The 1.3-liter engine was retained but fitted with an all-synchromesh 4-speed gearbox and optional overdrive. The overdrive was engaged by a switch in the center of the gear lever rather than a stalk on the steering column. Cars destined for markets outside the United States were still fed by the twin 1¼-inch SU carburetors and pushing 70 hp. The U.S.-spec cars with the solo Stromberg carb were barely scratching out 50 hp. Again, don't forget that at this time, U.S. carmakers were building cars with six times the engine displacement and eight times the horsepower.

During the time that the new car was being designed, the press was no longer sugar-coating its opinions of the swing-axle rear suspension. Words such as "frightening" were used and it was said to be the single element that detracted from an otherwise good car.

The revised suspension in the Mark IV was a simple variation on the old design simply to keep costs down. It still featured the transverse leaf spring, but it was allowed to pivot on top of the axle housing. This minor improvement reduced the dramatic camber changes substantially and helped to reduce roll stiffness. The car now had mild understeer and the rear "bucking" was gone

The new car came priced at only a few hundred dollars more than the previous Mark 3. The enthusiast media sang the praises of the new car as *Autocar* said, "A very much more civilized car . . . very pleasant to drive."

The next three years saw very few changes. A chin spoiler and reclining seats were added in 1973, but the wire wheels were dropped. In 1974, a factory tonneau cover was included. One of Spitfire's chief competitors, the Austin-Healey Sprite, was dropped from production in 1971. Sales had declined as development of the car had slowed and Leyland no longer wanted to pay a royalty to Donald Healey for each car sold.

Meanwhile in the United States, exhaust emissions legislation left the Spitfire gasping for air and sapped for power. By 1973, the car could barely muster 48 hp and 0-60 mph took longer than 16 seconds. It was 2 seconds slower than the Mark 3's 14 seconds flat!

1500

To maintain face and keep some semblance of performance in its popular sports car; the 1.5-liter engine was rushed to market in 1973. It was, in fact, a stroked version of the 1,296-cc engine migrated over from the 1500 sedan. To achieve the new displacement, stroke was increased from 76 to 87.5 mm. In U.K. spec (meaning non-U.S.), compression was boosted to 9.0:1 and it was fed by twin SU HS2-type carbs. The result was 71 hp at 5,500 rpm and 82 ft-lbs of torque. From a marketing perspective, the greater displacement was a perceived benefit; however, horsepower was effectively unchanged.

The gains were not nearly as robust in the U.S. market. Still burdened by the federal emissions mandates, the dual SU setup was dropped in favor of a single

The interior of the 1500 remained virtually unchanged over its final run except for some luxury or appearance upgrades. These included the addition of a sportier Moto-Lita steering wheel, thicker carpets, and optional hound's-tooth seat inserts. (Photo Courtesy Andy Robinson)

The wood fascia carried over throughout the rest of Spitfire's run. The look harkened back to the car's sporting roots. By this time, most manufacturers had begun the change to molded-plastic dashboards with the exception of Fiat's 124 Spider. (Photo Courtesy Andy Robinson)

Styling on the Spitfire was always an evolution rather than a revolution. Although bigger and 300 pounds heavier, the body lines can be traced back to the original Mark 2. By the end of the run, the 1,493-cc and all its anti-pollution gear had sapped power to just 71 bhp. (Photo Courtesy George Krause)

Through 1978, the Spitfire sported chrome bumpers front and rear. For 1979 and 1980, the new black rubber bumpers with large, energy-absorbing overriders were added. All of the safety and anti-smog equipment packed another 100 pounds onto the car. By 1979, the Spitfire tipped the scales at 1,875 pounds (850 kg). (Photo Courtesy George Krause)

Leyland had stopped investing development money in the Spitfire by the late 1970s. The only changes came when forced by new legislative rules such as the black energy-absorbing noses used on the 1979 and 1980 models. By this point, the Spitfire cockpit was the most nicely trimmed in the history of the car. An SCCA championship dash plaque adorned every fascia. Also visible here is the overdrive switch in the center of the shift knob. (Photo Courtesy Doug Stein)

Zenith-Stromberg unit and compression was dropped to 7.5:1. As a result, this detuned version of the 1500 delivered an anemic 57 hp.

Although the 1500 badge did not appear until 1975, all U.S. Mark IV cars from 1973 on featured the 1,493-cc engine. Once again, times were tight at Triumph. Just as the 1500 debuted in the market, the coffers were again empty, as British Leyland became a nationalized company.

Nationalizing of companies was a very common thing in Britain at this time. The economy was struggling and labor strife was quite common. The concept was to take an unhealthy company and merge it with a healthy company to pull it up. Unfortunately, the opposite happened and the healthy company became unhealthy.

No significant changes were made to this final iteration of the project originally known as the Bomb. The majority

The GT6 Mark 1 was unveiled in the fall of 1966. From the time that the Spitfire was launched, a GT version had always been on the boards, even though they were tenuous boards. However, when the 1,996-cc engine became available, a star was born.

CHAPTER 6: The Bomb Goes Off

The look of the first GT6 is unmistakably linked to the Spitfire Mark 2 and the cars shared many components inside and out. The GT6 Mark 2 received the same changes to the front bumper of the Spitfire: the raised nose to meet safety specifications.

The GT6 was not simply a hardtop version of the Spitfire. From every angle, Michelotti's design was sleek, sexy, and pure GT car. It was dubbed "the poor man's E-Type" because of the fastback design with an opening rear hatch.

of resources went into keeping the car buoyant in the all-important U.S. market. After all, 80 percent of all Spitfire sales were in the United States. This meant constantly chasing the emissions regulations to keep the car in compliance and various cosmetic appearance changes such as hound's-tooth fabric inserts in the seats, new steering wheels, and a switch gear brought over from TR7.

In August 1980, the last Spitfire 1500 rolled off the Canley assembly line after 91,137 were built. A grand total of 314,342 Spitfires were built during its five versions and 18 triumphant years. The Canley plant was closed shortly thereafter.

GT6

If the media was considered prophetic when predicting the potential success of the Spitfire, it must be considered clairvoyant when it comes to the GT6. In 1962, the original Spitfire was called Spitfire 4. This led many in the press to quip, "Will there be a Spitfire 6?" Triumph, however, had no plans for a 6-cylinder model and did not begin work on one in earnest until two years later.

Drawing a conclusion for a 6-cylinder model is really quite simple. If the Spitfire was a derivative of the 4-cylinder Herald and if the Vitesse was the sibling car to the Herald with a 6-cylinder engine, then it is obvious that the same 6-cylinder engine should fit into the Spitfire engine bay. Triumph, however, did not approach it that way.

To accommodate the longer and taller 6-cylinder, the one-piece tilting hood received an elongated bulge running nearly all the way to the nose of the car. This is the GT6 Plus badge, as it was called in the U.S. market. It was Mark 2 to the rest of the world.

A GT version of the Spitfire was envisioned virtually from the start of the program. Once a finished Spitfire 4 was available, it was sent to Michelotti's studios for concepting. Later in 1963, a prototype was returned for evaluation. Unfortunately, the added weight of the new hardtop proved to be too much for the 1,147-cc mill and the project was put on hold.

From its inception, Harry Webster had envisioned a closed version of the Spitfire and he proposed it to Triumph brass on several occasions. It was a difficult sell because of the additional cost to build and the ever-restrictive cash situation. In addition, the projected additional weight would have been a burden on the then-standard 63-hp 4-cylinder engine. You cannot take an upmarket luxury coupe to market that cannot get out of its own way.

While the dithering continued, Webster asked Michelotti to draw up a concept of a GT version of the Spitfire using as much of the existing bodywork as possible. In 1963, Michelotti built a fastback prototype on an unmodified car. Everything from the doors forward remained the same and even significant portions of the aft section of

Just as with the Spitfire, the opening front clip of the GT6 provided incomparable access to the engine and supporting elements. The 1,998-cc inline 6 delivered 95 hp and 117 ft-lbs of torque. Not only was the 6-cylinder designation a benefit to the making of a GT car, the extra power was needed to compensate for the additional weight of the hardtop.

Twin Stromberg 150CD carburetors delivered the fuel-and-air mixture to the heart of the GT6. Fuel economy was rated at 26 mpg, provided you kept your foot out of it. The 0-60–mph times were charted at 10.5 seconds with the quarter-mile covered in 18 seconds.

CHAPTER 6: The Bomb Goes Off

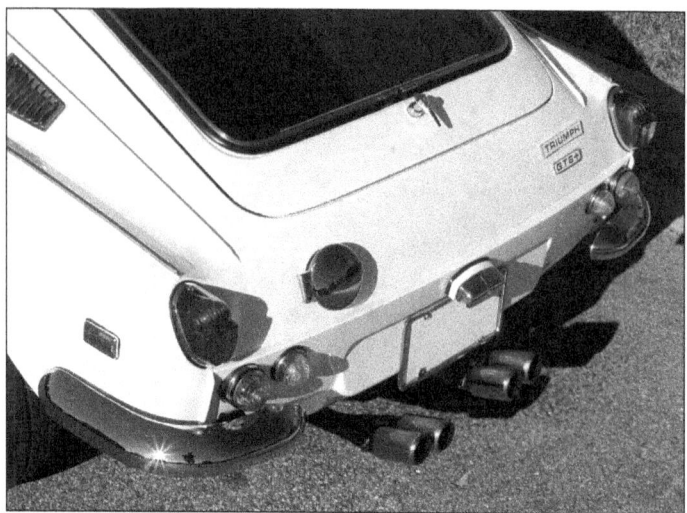

The rear panel of the GT was distinctive and the oversized fuel filler gave the car a sense of performance. The Mark 2 rear became a little busier with the additional signal lights, but it still looked good.

The most significant changes to the second-generation GT came at the rear of the car, but it wasn't only cosmetic. The rear suspension was reengineered using Rotoflex driveshaft couplings and new lower wishbones to cure the handling ills encountered during spirited driving.

The rear hatch allowed easy access to the 14.2 cubic feet of cargo space. Loading and unloading was fairly easy, but given the shape of the space, smaller, soft-sided bags were recommended to maximize usable space.

The roofline and rear section of the GT6 made the styling work so well. Much like the coupe version of the Karmann-Ghia, the GT6 flows far better than the convertible. The stamped steel wheels and Rostyle hubcaps were frequently replaced with Minilite-style aluminum wheels. (Photo Courtesy Alessandro Maschi)

In 1961, the XK-E was introduced simultaneously in roadster GT trim. When looking at the GT6, it is impossible not to draw a comparison to the Jaguar coupe. Although the GT6 did not officially launch until five years after the E-type, Michelotti was working on plans for a GT version of the Spitfire within a year after its debut in 1962. (Photo Courtesy Classic Car Garage)

If the roadster version was beautiful, the lines of the fixed-head coupe were simply sublime. From stem to stern, there is nothing about it that does not flow. The car has all the same features and performance of the open version, making the hatchback version a true Grand Touring car. In 1966, a 2+2 version was offered with four seats. The wheelbase was lengthened to accommodate the additional passengers and the roofline was raised for greater headroom. Unfortunately, the lines on the 2+2 version are not as elegant. (Photo Courtesy Classic Car Garage)

CHAPTER 6: The Bomb Goes Off

In the U.S. market the Mark 1 and Mark 2 versions both had a peak output of 95 hp. For 1968, the Mark 2 (shown) made 104 hp in the rest of the world thanks to a better-flowing head proven in the TR5/TR250. Alas, U.S. pollution regulations required a de-tuned version of the 1,996-cc engine.

The car was always envisioned as a luxury sports GT car so the interior received nicer appointments than its sibling, the Spitfire. These included a full-width wood-veneer fascia for the dashboard, full carpets, and nicely stitched seats and door panels.

The front bumper on the GT6 Plus (shown here in European designation as the Mark 2) was raised simultaneously on the Spitfire in accordance with new anti-crash legislation. Small louvers were added to the sides of the hood and on the rear buttresses. (Photo Courtesy Alessandro Maschi)

the Spitfire were used. Nothing ever came of it because the performance was grossly inadequate given the extra weight of the GT version.

One year later, the prototype was fitted with the Vitesse 1.6-liter 6-cylinder; however, at just 70 hp it did not scream GT. Moreover, that engine was about to be scrapped in favor of a more powerful 2.0-liter unit in development. At this point, the 2.0-liter Spitfire GT project remained a possibility and test cars were being assessed. That is until MG launched the MGB GT in the fall of 1965. Once again, Triumph reacted quickly and the GT6 was unveiled in October 1966.

The new car never had a secretive nickname and was known as GT6 from the get-go. As instructed, it shared the same wheelbase and suspension as its Spitfire sibling. In fact, it shared a significant amount of sheet metal and components.

The 1,998-cc engine with dual Zenith-Stromberg carburetors and 9.5:1 compression was bolted to an all-synchromesh 4-speed transmission with optional overdrive. The transmission came over from the Vitesse but was given first-gear mesh. This combination produced 95 hp and 117 ft-lbs of torque. Its 60 mph could be achieved in 12 seconds and the car had a top speed of 106 mph. It was more than befitting for a true GT car.

Because of the additional weight, stopping power had to be increased so the 9-inch front discs were replaced with 9.7-inch discs; its 8-inch drums replaced the 7-inch drums at the rear. The 13-inch stamped steel or wire wheels were optional. Spitfire's lightning-quick steering ratio had to be reduced because of the additional weight at the front end. Even so, it was plenty responsive.

From the very start, the GT6 was designed to be much more than just a 6-cylinder Spitfire. The interior received the luxury treatment with full carpets, padded door panels, and a center armrest over the parking brake. The seats were longer to provide more thigh support along with padded side bolsters.

The polished walnut dashboard put the large speedometer and tachometer in front of the driver with ancillary gauges and switches at the center. The passenger-side parcel shelf and grab handle were retained from the Spitfire. The rear cargo compartment boasted 14 cubic feet of space and was also fully trimmed along with a finished wood floor. To make the cargo space work, the Spitfire fuel tank was redesigned and relocated to the right side of the car.

Outside, the car was as sleek and sassy as the original Spitfire with profile styling somewhat reminiscent of the Jaguar E-Type coupe. The elongated bulge down the center of the hood was certainly similar to the famous big cat and also very necessary to accommodate the taller, longer engine. The rear's end panel was taken directly from the

The year 1970 saw the introduction of the final version of the GT6. Now known as Mark 3 around the world, the redesign brought the styling elements of the body in line with the rest of the Triumph line. This was primarily the rear panel used on the Spitfire Mark IV and Stag. The competition-style fuel cap was downsized and relocated to the left-rear fender. This studio shot also shows the new steel wheels with stamped fins. (Photo Courtesy British Motor Industry Heritage Trust)

Spitfire, except for the repositioned fuel filler. The fuel cap looked larger and more sporting in this presentation.

It is not a stretch to see how the styling of the coupe's roofline was derived when compared to the successful Le Mans Spitfires. The race cars of 1964 were modeled directly from the original Spitfire GT concept car.

The new car hit the market at £985 ($3,000), putting the GT6 smack-dab in the middle of its competitors. The MGB GT was priced just over £1,000, the Spitfire cost £750, and the TR4A cost £1,029.

The press reacted as expected, loving the look, the engine, and its power but still having difficulty coming to terms with the swing-axle rear suspension. All the same adjectives used to describe the rear-end hop and wheel spin were used on the GT6. However, the criticism was much more severe because the additional power from the 6 accentuated the problems.

Interior and exterior styling received mixed reviews. The common complaints were that the interior was too cramped and ventilation was poor. In fact, it could become downright sauna-like and opening the windows was the only relief. Nevertheless, the GT6 was an instant sales success. In 1966, 1,434 units were produced followed by 7,366 in 1967 and 7,018 in 1968.

As sales success continued to build, Triumph announced the GT6 Mark 2, known as the GT6 Plus for the U.S. market, in October 1968. This new model outwardly incorporated many of the cosmetic changes seen in the Spitfire Mark 3, but the main goal of the new model was to erase the blemishes of the first car (mainly the rear suspension) and make the GT a real touring car.

The transverse leaf spring was retained but modified with the addition of lower wishbones attached to the frame and wheel uprights. The new cast-iron lowers effectively turned the leaf spring into an upper wishbone creating a dual-wishbone setup of sorts. Axles were changed to half-shafts with a flexible rubber coupling that arrested the wildly dramatic changes in camber and made for a smoother, neutral-handling car.

Externally, the GT6 received the Spitfire Mark 3 nose along with new engine-cooling louvers located just behind the front wheels. Functional louvers were also placed just behind the rear-quarter windows to aid in cockpit ventilation along with two round, gimbaled, fresh-air vents in the dashboard. The U.S. version was available with the controversial Rostyle wheel covers. A rear-window defogger was also standard equipment.

Under the hood, the non-U.S. versions received a boost in performance when the TR5/TR250 head was fitted to the GT6. This resulted in 104 hp and 117 ft-lbs of torque. The increased power shaved 2 full seconds off the 0-60-mph time. Alas, America's GT6 Plus retained the old 95-hp powerplant to meet the new emissions standards.

Despite these positive and welcomed changes, sales of the new GT began to wobble at the end of 1969. The GT6 Mark 2/GT6 Plus needed an infusion of excitement and the

At the front, the distinctive center hood bulge was planed to give it a lower profile and the two banks of louvers near the firewall were deleted. To meet federal front-impact regulations, the supplemental rubber bumpers were added and, despite being ugly, were styled in the least offensive way. (Photo Courtesy Richard Spiegelman)

Other cosmetic changes to the Mark 3 were redesigned and flush-mounted door handles. The chrome strips atop the fenders were dropped in favor of a smoother, more modern look. The same goes for the turn signal and marker lights. (Photo Courtesy Richard Spiegelman)

only real option was to restyle the appearance. The new Mark 3 was announced in October of 1970 and brought the new version of the GT6 in series with the Spitfire Mark IV. This time the entire world knew the car as the Mark 3.

The new GT6 received the nose and flat tail panel of the Mark IV Spitfire. The hood bulge was planed and made wide so that it was not as pronounced, and all functional engine-cooling louver vents were gone. The fender-top seams on the hood were also removed but remained in place on the rear fenders. The Stag-inspired rear panel required the fuel door to be moved to the left-rear fender and the rear hatch was redesigned to match the new rear treatment. The fuel filler was moved from the rear panel to the left-side fender and the cap was made flush with the bodywork. More modern, flush-mount door handles were also brought over from cousin Spitfire.

The Mark 3 was easily the most handsome of the GT6 family, but despite its good looks, British Leyland seemed content to let the car wither on the vine.

In the epilogue of a 1971 GT comparison article featuring the GT6 Mark 3, Opel GT, MGB GT, Datsun 240Z, and Fiat 124 Sport Coupe, *Road & Track* speculated as follows, "We sincerely hope England will be able to get off her duff, produce some competitive cars again, and challenge the other countries. We have reason to believe that British Leyland does intend to keep building sports cars and to come up not only with new designs but to realign the product mix of MG, Triumph, and Jaguar. One of these new products, we would predict, will be a medium-price GT replacing both the B and GT6." Unfortunately, it appears that *Road & Track*'s crystal ball was a bit fogged, as none of this came to be.

The GT6 Mark 3 was superior to stablemate MGB GT in price and performance, but it now faced formidable competition in the form of the new Datsun 240Z and, to some degree, the Opel GT. All four cars were competitively priced in the neighborhood of $3,500, but stiffening U.S. emissions laws and lack of development suffocated the GT6 out of existence.

Nothing of significance changed mechanically for the Mark 3. More emissions-friendly Stromberg 150 CDSE carburetors were fitted to the non-U.S.–spec cars. Horsepower was rated at 98 at 5,300 rpm and 108 ft-lbs of torque. The 0–60 speed was unaffected and top speed was 112 mph. By 1972, horsepower output for the U.S.-spec smog model was just 79 bhp. During that same year the GT6 was fitted with the Spitfire Mark IV's new suspension system, which was not superior to the swing arm/wishbone setup but was cheaper to produce. Alas, it was too little too late and sales continued to decline. Just 2,745 cars were sold in 1973 and it was no longer feasible to build the car.

Seven years and one month from its debut, the GT6 died unceremoniously in November 1973 after a total of 41,000 units were produced. The Spitfire carried on for another seven years.

Inside the cabin, little was changed for the Mark 3 except for new modern switches that were being rolled out across the entire line. The wood-veneer fascia remained a stalwart of its Spitfire origins. (Photo Courtesy Richard Spiegelman)

CHAPTER 6: The Bomb Goes Off

CHAPTER 7

TRIUMPH ON TRACK

The Works TR2 team after the finish of the 1955 24 Hours of Le Mans. Car no. 29, driven by Bert Hadley and Ken Richardson; car no. 68, driven by Leslie Brooke and Mortimer Morris-Goodall; and car no. 28, driven by Bob Dickson and Ninian Sanderson. The cars were entered as prototypes and were fitted with Girling and Dunlop disc brakes. Finishing in 14th, 15th, and 19th places, it was a good showing for the team as they went head-to-head with MGA prototypes. The race was marred by a tragic accident when a Mercedes-Benz launched into the crowd, killing 80. Triumph did not return to Le Mans until 1959. (Photo Courtesy Revs Institute/George Phillips Collection)

Triumph's place in racing history can be likened to the tag line of comedian Rodney Dangerfield: no respect. It may seem flippant to characterize Triumph's racing legacy in such a way, but it is not completely unfounded.

Consider Triumph's peers of the era: Jaguar, Austin-Healey, MG, and even Lotus. They are more frequently associated with racing success than Triumph. The burly Big Healeys and the plucky Healey Sprites campaigned regularly at both Le Mans and Sebring. There was Jaguar's mini dynasty, winning Le Mans three times in the iconic D-Type Jaguar and Aston Martin's incredible DBRs that won Le Mans nine times with the greatest drivers of the day.

Given the fact that Triumph had only intermittent Le Mans entries, the truth of the matter is that Triumph was very successful in European and North American rallying, Le Mans, and endurance racing. The Triumph brand was incredibly prolific in winning Sports Car Club of America (SCCA) championships.

In the United States, Healey enjoyed great success in SCCA racing, winning national championships in D-, E-, and F-Production classes in the 1960s. The last SCCA championship came in 1965 with a 100-6 in E-Production class. And prior to success on the track, a streamlined Austin-Healey 100 set several records on the Bonneville Salt Flats in 1953.

As the most prolific manufacturer of the group, it's no surprise that MG was involved in virtually every form of motorsport. Shortly after the doors first opened at the MG Car Company in Oxford, cars were in competition. Most notable was the 1931 C-Type that enthusiasts campaigned with company assistance. In the United States the MGA and MGB are synonymous with SCCA racing. Of course, I would be remiss if I did not mention the 1939 MG EX135 streamliner that achieved 200 mph at Bonneville. Triumph did not attempt speed runs at Bonneville.

Jaguar's racing resume casts the longest shadow of all with decades of success that carries on today. The sporting

XKs had nearly instant success on the track and paved the way for the pure performance of the C-Type and amazing D-Type. It won Le Mans with the C-Type in 1951 and 1953 and the D-Type captured the top step of the podium in 1955, 1956, and 1957. Jaguar's place in racing history was cemented from then on.

Triumph's racing pedigree is certainly on equal footing with Austin-Healey and MG, if not Jaguar as well. Triumph claimed multiple podiums at Le Mans over two decades and was the rally car of choice in the 1950s. SCCA starting grids across the United States were heavily populated with TRs and Spitfires from the 1950s through the 1970s and they are popular vintage racers today. The origins of Triumph's racing legacy began as rapidly as the first production sports car.

This is a pretty stout resume considering Standard-Triumph's on-again-off-again commitment to motorsports. Despite being continually short on resources and over-matched on budgets, Triumph's achievements in rallying and road racing are a testament to the heart of the people behind the program. And behind the wheel.

It seems that many people don't think a lot about the big racing victories when looking back on Triumph's history. However, if you are old enough to have been watching Triumph through the 1950s, 1960s, and 1970s you will remember that racing success was a regular part of its advertising and marketing. Triumph's road car success can be directly tied to its racing success.

IN THE BEGINNING

Triumph did not have a Competitions department in 1952 and had no interest in competition, particularly with Sir John Black as managing director. That all changed shortly after Ken Richardson's successful run at Jabbeke Road in Belgium in 1953. Richardson's history and affinity for racing put him in the position to immediately recognize what was happening when customers were purchasing the new TR2 for competition. Even prior to the debut of the TR2, Richardson had taken note of privateers entering Triumphs, such as the Renown, in the Monte Carlo Rally and placing well.

Car no. 29, driven by Ken Richardson and Bert Hadley, passing beneath the famous Dunlop tire bridge entering Tertre Rouge Corner. Despite reaching top speeds near 115 mph, it wasn't enough to compete with Jaguars hitting 180 mph and lapping half a minute quicker. Richardson and Hadley finished 15th overall. (Photo Courtesy Revs Institute/Rodolfo Mailander Collection)

It's worth noting that Triumph did have an interest in competition with the 1934 Dolomite Straight Eight. Under the stewardship of Donald Healey, it could have laid the groundwork for a rich motorsports history. Unfortunately, Triumph's financial woes in the latter half of the decade nipped that in the bud.

The first factory-owned car to compete officially was a TR2 loaned to *Autosport* editor Gregor Grant to run in the 1954 Lyons-Charbonnières rally in France. It was a stock TR2 and Grant finished 2nd in class. He followed with another 2nd in class at the Dutch Tulip Rally. Around this same time, a rally driver named Johnny Wallwork was the overall winner of the RAC Rally in a stock TR2, beating full-on factory teams from Sunbeam and Ford.

Following that success, Triumph had a factory Competitions department with Richardson at the helm. He occupied a small corner of the factory and borrowed whatever mechanics he could find. Also at this point, Black was gone and Alick Dick was now in charge. Dick was very much pro-motorsports and gave Richardson two goals: the French Alpine Rally in Marseille, France, and the Mille Miglia in Brescia, Italy. It was suddenly apparent that the upstart department would be supporting two different tracks: rallying and road racing.

Richardson was a good rally driver in his own right, but there was no way he could lead the department *and* drive the cars. During his seven-year tenure Richardson managed a revolving door of drivers and co-drivers. It is said that he often played favorites by putting his buddies behind the wheel rather than the best driver available.

Dick was also aware of his engineering department's connections to Dutch rally champ Maurice Gatsonides. "Gatso," as he was known, had won the 1952 Alpine Cup and the 1953 Monte Carlo rally. He spent the next four years driving for Triumph, winning the Alpine Cup in 1954 and 1956.

From 1954 to 1961 Richardson managed rally and road racing versions of the TR2, TR3, TR3A, and the special TR3S and TRS Le Mans cars. The latter are the most interesting cars from the period because Richardson's Competitions department did not really do a great deal to the cars. Richardson believed that the cars were strong enough to win right off the assembly line. Engines were not specially tuned nor were brakes or suspensions uprated. He did always use

The Richardson/Hadley entry in the Esses, 1955. All three Triumph entries ran the rainswept event with canvas tonneau covers. In the background is a Panhard X86 that crashed out midway through the race. (Photo Courtesy Revs Institute/Rodolfo Mailander Collection)

the freshest cars off the line with the most recently used cars being sold off and replaced.

In the early days, Richardson was correct; the TR2 and TR3 2-liter was stout enough to run rallies with the other cars in class. Gatsonides finished 2nd in class at the 1954 French Alpine Rally and 7th in class at the 1954 Mille Miglia. Richardson achieved 2nd in class at the 1955 Tulip Rally and 1st in class at the Liège-Rome-Liège event.

In addition to Richardson and Gatsonides, the stable of rally drivers included Paddy Hopkirk, John Waddington, Rob Slotemaker, French ladies' rally champ Annie Soisbault, and BMC driver Nancy Mitchell. TR2s, TR3s, and TR3As were regular participants in the same events through the years: RAC, French Alpine, Monte Carlo, Lyon-Charbonnières, Liege-Rome-Liege. All had varying levels of success in the events with a handful of 1sts and many 2nds, 3rds, 4ths, and 5ths.

Again, the Works rally cars were essentially production cars with little or no prep work with the exception of some Lucas driving lights and a fitted hardtop when required. Of course, there were factory developments that helped the Works cars maintain an edge such as standard Girling front disc brakes on TR3s and the larger 2,138-cc engine that boosted horsepower to 105.

The Works road racing cars began similarly to the rally cars coming straight off the assembly line and into competition. No engine or gearbox changes, no suspension or brake upgrades, not even a roll bar. However, the

The new TRS turned out nicely on the grid at Le Mans in 1960. The no. 29 car was driven by Peter Bolton and Ninian Sanderson. It finished the race a distant 59 miles behind teammates Keith Ballisat and Marcel Becquart when valve issues robbed the car of power. (Photo Courtesy Revs Institute/Albert R Bochroch Collection)

development trajectory of road racing cars was rapid and, by the end, radical.

As with the rally cars, the birth of the road racing effort came about because of the success of a privateer in a Triumph. In 1954 Edgar Wadsworth, a journeyman racer of some means, took a street-stock TR2 to Le Mans and finished 15th overall. Of course, this garnered the attention of everyone at the factory. Richardson and company immediately began working toward the 1955 Le Mans event with the goal of a three-car factory entry.

Three TR2s were pulled from the assembly line in sequence and readied for the race. On the outside, all three cars were stripped of their bumpers and windscreens. They ran with a canvas tonneau covering the cockpit and the ubiquitous diminutive wind deflector in front of the driver. Lucas driving lamps were mounted in the recessed mouth on the front apron. It was a great look, but unfortunately the large lamps blocked airflow to the radiator.

The drivetrain was not changed at all. At the corners, all three cars were fitted with experimental disc brake systems. In fact, two systems were being tested in the race: a Girling front brake and a Dunlop four-wheel brake system. All three cars were painted British Racing Green.

During the race, the TR2s were no match for the mighty Jaguars and Mercedes-Benzes that bested the newcomers by 60 mph on the Mulsanne Straight. But Triumph wasn't there to race the Jags and Mercedes-Benzes. The main competition came from the prototype MGAs that were also debuting at this race. The MGs had aluminum bodies and were powered by the 1.5-liter engines.

Richardson and his team were pleased with the results. The Triumphs finished 14th, 15th, and 19th against the MG results of 12th, 17th, and DNF. In addition, both brake systems were successful and this test was the catalyst for the introduction of the Girling system on TR3s.

Race fans will recall that the 1955 Le Mans was marred by the crash of Pierre Levegh's Mercedes-Benz 300 SLR, killing him and 80 spectators. Mercedes-Benz withdrew from the race with Juan Manuel Fangio in the lead. Mike Hawthorn went on to win the race overall in the spectacular Jaguar D-Type. After the tragedy, Mercedes-Benz withdrew from factory-sponsored motor racing. The self-imposed ban lasted into the 1980s.

Keith Ballisat and Marcel Becquart drove to a superb 9th overall in 1960. Theirs was the only car that didn't suffer from valve fatigue. Judging by the gentleman below the Cinzano sign, track safety was quite relaxed in those days. (Photo Courtesy Revs Institute/Karl Ludvigsen Collection)

CHAPTER 7: Triumph on Track

Despite being pleased with their results, Richardson and Triumph did not return to Le Mans for several years. The speed disparity between the production-based TR2s and the purpose-built racing cars was glaring. Richardson and Triumph remained steadfast in their commitment to running factory-stock powerplants. There was no sense in returning if they were only going to be embarrassed yet again.

That said, Alick Dick and chief engineer Harry Webster were bit by the racing bug. They began work on a plan to return to Le Mans. The goal was a car that looked like an existing production model but had a very special engine. The project was code named 20X.

It is pretty obvious that the code name was derived from "2-liter" and "experimental." However, today it is known by a completely different name, but I'll get back to the name in a minute. They went with a 2-liter engine because they had experience in that racing class. Double overhead cam engines were quite popular at this time, made fashionable by the Jaguar XKs and Ferraris. Dick wanted a DOHC performance engine that could be built economically enough, so that, if successful, it could be offered in a production road car. Of course, every automobile aficionado knows that performance and economy are rarely used in the same sentence.

The design needed to be simple. At the center of the engine was the cast-iron block, but the rest of the key components (sump, crankcase, and cylinder head) were cast aluminum. These pieces were stacked and held together by long bolts from the main bearing caps to the cylinder head. The cylinder head was a conventional design with the cams operating the coil-sprung valves. Single spark plugs were fitted into the semi-spherical combustion chambers.

The experimental powerplant was fed by two twin-choke SU carburetors. Most engine builders of the day would have more than likely selected twin-choke Weber carburetors for a performance application such as this. However, because SUs were fitted to the road cars and Triumph's philosophy was to have a clear link between its road cars and racing cars, there was no choice.

The final result was a 1,985-cc engine with five main bearings, a 90-mm bore, and a 78-mm stroke. The lump pro-

For 1964, Triumph entered three Spitfires in the 24 Hours of Le Mans. Only one of the three cars finished the race, coming 3rd in class and 21st overall. Drivers David Hobbs and Rob Slotemaker teamed up to bring ADU2B home after completing 272 laps with an average speed of 94.7 mph. Here, Hobbs is on the right, standing on the pitwall with his helmet. (Photo Courtesy British Motor Industry Heritage Trust)

duced a reliable 150 bhp at 6,500 rpm. Lump is an appropriate term because it was a large engine. At 438 pounds, it was only slightly lighter than the 1,991-cc production pushrod engines, but it was much larger.

About that code name. Access to the chain-driven camshaft adjustments and timing was covered by two rather pronounced domed castings. These castings were quite prominent and likened to the figure of a young movie starlet of the era, Norma Sykes, better known as Sabrina, who was generously endowed. The engine was nicknamed Sabrina after her and it stuck. The references to Sabrina apparently far outweighed 20X and at some point the engine was officially renamed Sabrina.

Meanwhile, in the street car department, work was starting on a successor for the TR3A. It would have been supremely synergistic for the new experimental racing engine to debut in the new model. Unfortunately they were not close. And there was no denying the sales success of the TR3A. The engine was mounted to a model dubbed the TR3S and readied for the 1959 Le Mans race.

The standard TR3 chassis was beefed up with a stronger rear axle and stiffer suspension. The frame was also

The 2-liter twin-cam engine was designed specifically for Triumph's return to Le Mans in 1959. Fueled by twin SU carburetors, the engine was heavier than the 2-liter wet-sleeve engine it was replacing, but it made more than 150 hp. Originally code named 20X, the engine became known as Sabrina because the bulbous cam covers were reminiscent of a movie starlet who possessed astonishing attributes.

It was hoped that the engine would prove itself on the track and that a production version could be developed for road cars. (Photo Courtesy Revs Institute/George Phillips Collection)

lengthened 6 inches to accommodate the Sabrina engine. The added length was fitted between the front axle and cockpit. Of course, to make it look like a production TR3A it needed a slight reworking of the body lines.

The car was made of fiberglass to save weight, which helped with making the racing car look like the street car. The main change was in the contour of the fender. For a person who doesn't know Triumphs very well, it was probably not noticeable. The cockpit was wrapped by a low-rise, slightly raked plexiglass windscreen that fared back to plexiglass side curtains. Again, all bumpers were removed and all three cars were British Racing Green. To tell the cars apart on the track the noses were painted different colors: red, white, and yellow.

The result was a sleek and racier-looking version of the TR3. Unfortunately, the experiment with the fiberglass body to save weight failed. In final race trim the TRS was actually heavier than its production-based brother. And the sleeker look did not result in better aerodynamics.

Three TRSs were prepped and sent to Le Mans in the summer of 1959. Despite being heavy and not terribly aerodynamic, the TRSs had better acceleration and top speed than their previous visit to the banks of the Sarthe. Unfortunately all three cars failed to finish.

Two of the TRSs retired as a result of the fan blades fragmenting and puncturing the cooling system. The third car was called in to remove the fan blades as a preventative measure and sent back out into the fray. With just two hours remaining on the clock, the oil pump failed and the car retired after attaining 7th place in class.

Overall, the weekend was a supreme disappointment and a public relations debacle for Triumph. However, the Sabrina engine proved itself.

Back at the Banner Lane facility, plans to put the Sabrina engine into limited production were beginning to gel. The

Replica of XHP939 originally driven by Ninian Sanderson and Claude Dubois. The car made it 9 hours into the 1959 event before the radiator was fatally punctured. All three entries were powered by the Sabrina engine; they looked like the TR3A road car but had a 6-inch-longer wheelbase. The cars also had many fiberglass panels to reduce weight and the Perspex wraparound windscreen. None of the cars finished the race. (Photo Courtesy James Pitt)

goal was to put the engine into 1,000 units of the newly designed replacement for the TR3A. Unfortunately, the final direction was not yet determined. Michelotti had delivered both the Zoom and Zest prototypes; the Zoom was finally chosen to become the TR4.

To introduce the newly minted body to the public, four fiberglass versions were created to fit onto the TR3S frame. The chassis was modified with a wider track and rack-and-pinion steering was added. Nothing else from the TR3S was changed and off to the 1960 Le Mans they went. Three cars competed and finished the 24 hours, but speeds were not impressive.

Despite Standard-Triumph being under immense financial pressure, the same three cars were entered in the 1961 24-hours event. Richardson's team was able to squeeze five additional horses from the Sabrina engine and it paid off. The cars finished 9th, 11th, and 15th to capture the team prize.

Sadly, the celebrations were short-lived. In a cash-saving move, Leyland shut down the Competitions department and Richardson was dismissed at the same time. But Triumph was back at Le Mans in four years with a new car.

NEW OWNERSHIP, NEW CARS, NEW RACING EFFORT

The champagne on the podium from the 1961 race was barely dry when Leyland shuttered the Competitions department. Ken Richardson was gone, as was any trace of Triumph's history in competition. All records were destroyed and the cars were sold off.

Despite the front-office political and financial machinations that brought the Richardson chapter to a close, Harry Webster had never given up on the idea of keeping Triumph active in competition. Later that same year he tapped recently hired engineer Graham Robson to help re-launch the Works department with the title of Competitions Secretary. Apart from his engineering skills, Robson was an accomplished rally driver for cross-town rival Sunbeam.

Webster provided Robson with four newly minted TR4s and a work space in the former tractor facility. Of course, they had no budget, no outside resources, no history to go on, and only a few loaned mechanics. The two men agreed

For the 1960 Le Mans race, four new TRS racing models were produced using the chassis from the 1959 car but fitting a new body. Clearly modeled from the Michelotti Zoom prototype, the body was made primarily of fiberglass to save weight. The 150 horses of the Sabrina mill were harnessed by disc brakes fitted to all four wheels. (Photo Courtesy British Motor Industry Heritage Trust)

The new TRS Le Mans car was modeled after Michelotti's Zoom concept well before the street version was ready. The fiberglass bodies were mounted on the frame from the old TR3S that competed in 1959. Of course, it was powered by the 1,985-cc twin-cam Sabrina engine. (Photo Courtesy James Pitt)

to a limited schedule of just five rallies for the new program.

The four cars were stripped down with two goals in mind: make them stronger and make them lighter. Frames were beefed up, superfluous trim and comfort items were removed, and steel body panels were replaced with aluminum panels.

Over the next two years, the cars were campaigned with limited success. The upstart Triumph Works team had to make do with the small trickle of money that Webster was able to wring out of the corporate coffers. They tried everything they could think of to boost performance including

The cockpit shown here is standard for the street version. The original Le Mans competition cars had only a single large tachometer and the bare minimum of gauges. Switches were unlabeled as they were in most competition cars of the day. This vintage racer features a roll bar and seatbelts. The original Le Mans cars were not equipped with either. (Photo Courtesy James Pitt)

Weber carburetors and limited-slip differentials. Ultimately, Robson and company were unable to coax enough power from the standard 2.2-liter engine to match the might of the 2.9-liter Big Healeys. The TR4 rally efforts were scrapped after 1964.

All the while, Webster still had a bad taste in his mouth from the way the TRS program fizzled after Le Mans. He was determined to return to road racing and Le Mans. Unfortunately, the new Works TR4 program revealed that an entry in the 2-liter class would be pure folly, so he turned his attention to the smaller-displacement class.

In 1963, work began on prepping the Spitfire for Le Mans with the goal of competing in the 1-liter class in 1964. The first order of business was to boost output from the 63-hp 1,147-cc engine. The goal was 100 hp. Dual twin-choke Webers were fitted along with a tuned exhaust and a cast-iron eight-port cylinder head with oversize valves. An aluminum version of the eight-port head was also considered, but there was concern over durability.

For many privateer racers, the TR3 proved to be the car of choice because it was powerful, durable, relatively inexpensive, and fairly easy to modify. In the 1950s, drivers frequently raced in short sleeves and the equivalent of a polo helmet; cars did not have roll bars or even seatbelts.

This accident at the 1956 Redwood Empire amateur race in Arcata, California, claimed the life of William Howard "Pete" Snell. Another amateur racer, Dr. Howard Snively, was the course physician and after seeing how poorly the existing crash helmets worked, he began serious efforts to do something about it. Within a year and with help from the SCCA, the Snell Foundation was born and by 1959 the first Snell standards were implemented. The Snell number certifications for helmets continue to this day. (Photo Courtesy Revs Institute/William Hewitt Collection)

CHAPTER 7: Triumph on Track

Leslie Brooke and Jack Fairman in their Works TR2 at the start of the 1954 Mille Miglia. The duo finished 94th overall in a field of 483 cars. A second TR2 piloted by Ken Richardson and Maurice Gatsonides finished 27th overall. The 21st running of the world sports car championship was rerouted through Mantua, Italy, the last home of legendary driver Tazio Nuvolari, who had passed away just a year earlier. (Photo Courtesy Revs Institute/Rodolfo Mailander Collection)

The race-prepped 1,147-cc engine, ready for its debut at the 1964 24 Hours of Le Mans. To maximize power, an experimental 8-port cast-iron head was fitted, which resulted in 98 hp at 6,750 rpm. (Photo Courtesy Revs Institute/George Phillips Collection)

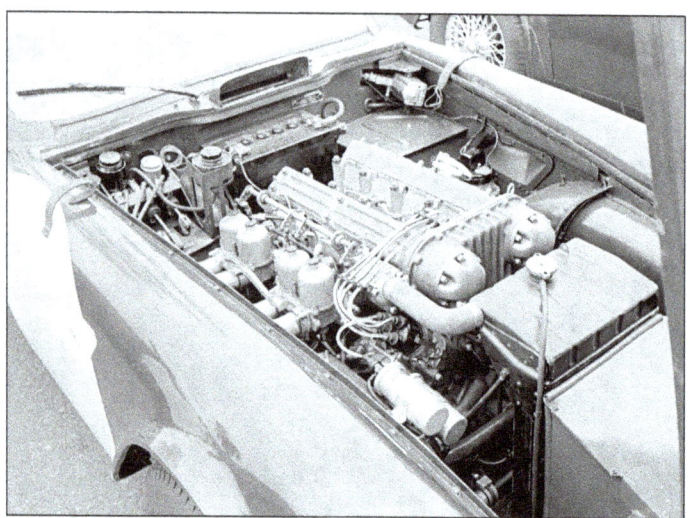

The factory sent four cars to Le Mans in 1961, but only three competed in the race. The cars were virtually identical to the 1960 entries with the exception of air vents on the front fenders. The valve issues in the Sabrina engine were solved and the cars ran strong to the finish. Keith Ballisat and Peter Bolton shared duties in 926 HP, finishing 9th overall.

Triumph captured the Manufacturer's Team trophy in 1961. The lead car completed one lap of the clock with an average speed of 98 mph and hit 130 mph on the Mulsanne Straight. Mission accomplished, Triumph dropped the TRS program and sold off the cars. (Photo Courtesy Revs Institute/Karl Ludvigsen Collection)

Power was channeled to the rear wheels through an all-synchro 4-speed gearbox scavenged from the TR4. Final output was rated at 98 hp and deemed good enough power, but top-end speeds and aerodynamics were still a question mark.

The TRS cars were heavy and decidedly not aerodynamic. To be competitive, this new Le Mans entry needed to maximize top-line speed on the 3.7-mile-long Mulsanne Straight. Enter Michelotti's GT-styling prototype. The long fastback-style roofline looked sleek enough for higher speeds and provided needed body rigidity. Of course, steel panels were replaced with aluminum and the cars were prepped for testing.

After rigorous speed and distance testing everyone was satisfied that the car was ready. Surprisingly, the factory-spec suspension and chassis delivered the best performance. Larger brakes were pulled from the TR4 and fitted to the race-spec Spitfires. Three cars were readied and sent to Le Mans for the 1964 event. Triumph's driver lineup included Rob Slotemaker, Bob Tullius, and David Hobbs.

THE MACAU SPITFIRE

Just before the Competitions department was shut down, a special race version of the Spitfire was commissioned at the behest of Walter Sulke, who was head of Standard-Triumph's distribution in Hong Kong.

The car was a special lightweight version of the Spitfire made just to compete in the Macau Grand Prix. The Macau Car, as it is known in the annals of Triumph history, was built from existing inventory of parts, not modified from an existing race car.

The Spitfire frame was fitted with an all-aluminum tub featuring an open cockpit and flat rear-deck area. Despite the open cockpit, only a driver's seat was fitted. An aluminum panel covered what would have been the passenger space on the left and a Perspex screen wrapped the driver's side to the right.

The Le Mans–style nose was bolted to the front. The most dramatic styling cue was the large "head fairing" behind the driver that was reminiscent of the D-Type Jaguars. This gave the experimental car an extremely exotic and aggressive look.

Under the long hood was the 109-hp version of the 1,147-cc engine mated to a GT6 gearbox and 4:11 gears at the rear end.

On November 28, 1965, Sulke drove the car to 3rd place in the Macau race. Because Triumph's Competitions department was shut down by this time, the car was returned to Coventry. In 1966, the car was shipped to California to be campaigned by Kas Kastner. After changing hands a number of times, the Macau Car is now part of a private collection.

Just as the Competitions department was shutting down, a special one-off lightweight race version of the Spitfire was commissioned at the behest of Walter Sulke, the head of Standard-Triumph's distribution in Hong Kong. The car was created just to compete in the Macau Grand Prix.
The Spitfire frame was fitted with an all-aluminum tub featuring an open cockpit and flat rear-deck area. The Le Mans–style nose was bolted to the front and a dramatic "head fairing" was fitted behind the driver. Under the long hood was the 109-hp version of the 1,147-cc engine mated to a GT6 gearbox and 4:11 gears at the rear end. Sulke drove the car to 3rd place in the Macau race. (Photo Courtesy Bernard Robinson, Courtesy of Ray Henderson)

Twin-choke Weber carburetors were used to help boost output and reach the needed 130 mph. Only one of the three cars entered finished the race; it had an average speed of just under 95 mph. The under–1,150-cc class was at a huge deficit on the Mulsanne Straight with the big V-8 and V-12 cars topping 200 mph. A testament to the rearward visibility and rearview mirrors. (Photo Courtesy Revs Institute/Karl Ludvigsen Collection)

Sadly, just a quarter of the way into the race distance, two of the cars had crashed out. The last entry, driven by Hobbs and Slotemaker, finished one lap off the clock with an average speed of 95 mph. This was good enough for a 3rd in-class finish behind two Alpine Renaults and well ahead of their chief rival, the Austin-Healey Sprite.

Back in Coventry, the damaged cars were repaired and readied for competition in 1965. Three cars were shipped to Florida for the 12 Hours of Sebring in March. The driver lineup included Bob Tullius and Charles Gates.

The 1965 endurance race is best remembered for a mega-monsoon that struck midway through the race, flooding the pit area. Despite all the standing water, the race was never stopped. This time only one Spitfire crashed out with the remaining cars finishing 2nd and 3rd in class behind Paddy Hopkirk's Austin-Healey Sprite. A successful weekend for sure.

In June, four homologated GT Spitfires were sent to France for the 24 Hours of Le Mans. For this event, the cast-iron heads were replaced with aluminum heads. The replacement heads were good for 109 hp and 140 mph on the Mulsanne Straight.

Two cars retired, including the Hobbs/Slotemaker entry, but the remaining two cars finished 1st and 2nd in class. It was a resounding success for Triumph and gratifying for Webster, who believed in the value of factory-supported motorsports.

The Le Mans race marked the end of the road for the official Competitions department. But Triumph went out on a high note.

RACING STATESIDE

It is well documented that privateers were able to get a lot more performance out of the Triumph powerplants than the factory Works team. Let's not forget that it was a privateer's success that put the wheels in motion for the creation of the Competitions department. Although Richardson kept everything stock, including the SU carburetors, he remained steadfast in capping revs at the factory-rated 5,500. A hotter cam, Weber carbs, and spinning the wet-sleeve 2.2-liter to 6,000 rpm was regularly delivering more than 100 bhp.

Automotive engine performance history is filled with lists of people who have an affinity for tuning a specific type of engine. Somehow these people magically relate to a particular engine better than anyone else and become

R. W. "Kas" Kastner leading the 1959 *Los Angeles Examiner* Grand Prix at Pomona in his TR3A. Kastner said that he was leaning so far out of the cockpit so he could see his front tires. The curbs at Pomona are quite large and could cause race-ending damage. Kastner went on to win the race and the SCCA Championship that year. (Photo Courtesy Kas Kastner)

Kastner in the Cal Sales garages as the newly crowned SCCA champion. Kastner is revered for his skill in tuning the Triumph wet-sleeve engines. He went on to a successful career in sailboat racing and race team management. He ran the Nissan IMSA program with driver Geoff Brabham. (Photo Courtesy Kas Kastner)

But it was Kas Kastner who was regularly piling up the trophies and championships in his TR2 and TR3. All the while supported by Cal Sales, for marketing purposes, of course. He understood the cars so well and he had a regular parade of racers coming to him for performance tips and performance parts. Speed parts and tuning became a nearly full-time side job for Kastner until a more formalized Triumph competitions program was forged.

For the TR3 and TR4 engines Kastner increased performance through a variety of proven tricks and techniques developed from experience. Heads were ported and polished to improve flow and then milled to increase compression to near 12:1. A shroud was installed on the radiator to aid cooling, which also aided in airflow to the carburetors. With the help of Dean Moon, Kastner was able to create a camshaft that delivered the best power curve to reliably produce 150 bhp. Even with the stock SUs.

Kastner was able to coax more power and reliability out of the wet-sleeve engines than anyone in history. Even the factory teams. He believed in thorough preparation and became known for his phrase, "Don't get beat by the equipment." Kastner was team manager for the first TR4 campaign at the 12 Hours of Sebring in 1961. (Photo Courtesy Kas Kastner)

synonymous with it. Ralph Moody on FE Fords, David Vizard on small-block Chevrolets, and Ed Pink on Hemi Elephants. Such is the case with R. W. "Kas" Kastner and Standard-Triumph.

Kastner was an employee of Cal Sales in Los Angeles. Cal Sales' owner Dorothy Deen (see the "Swallow Doretti" sidebar in Chapter 2) recognized the value of racing as a marketing tool for her fledgling Triumph dealership. Jaguar, MG, and even Ferrari were already prevalent on the West Coast and anything to trumpet the performance success of Triumph TR3s was welcomed.

Deen was able to get drivers such as Phil Hill and Richie Ginther to drive her TR3s at local events. Both Hill and Ginther went on to drive Formula 1, with Hill winning the Championship in 1961.

GRASS-ROOTS RACING GOES CORPORATE

Throughout 1960, Standard-Triumph was buying out its distributors to gain better control of the sales channels. Cal Sales was one of the most successful Triumph distributorships in the United States, selling more TR3s than any other outlet. Deen signed over Cal Sales in October and Kastner, now a factory employee, was told he could no longer race.

Racing was a big part of Triumph and Cal Sales success, and the U.S. arm of Standard-Triumph wanted to perpetuate this, so Kastner was asked how to go about it. Kastner and Triumph's New York–based advertising and public relations manager, Mike Cook, hatched a plan to go to Sebring with the new TR4.

In 1962, three hardtop TR4s were delivered to Kastner in California to prep for the 1963 12-Hours. To ensure maximum impact on the U.S. racing scene, Cook and Kastner invited current TR4 SCCA champions to drive in the race. This included Bob Tullius, Charlie Gates, Bruce Kellner, and Ed Diehl. U.K. headquarters insisted on experienced wheelmen and sent Le Mans TRS drivers Peter Bolton and Mike Rothschild.

Long after the sun set in central Florida, the Kastner-prepped TR4s finished 1st, 2nd, and 4th in class. The Triumphs were also the only complete team to finish the race. Shortly thereafter, Kastner was officially named Competitions Manager for Triumph U.S.

The 1965 Sebring TR4 campaigned by Kas Kastner in nearly American racing colors. As Kastner tells it, his crew was working around the clock to prep the stock TR4s pulled from the lot at Cal Sales. They had no time to properly paint the cars so one of the crew was dispatched to find blue paint. Proper blue paint proved to be elusive and all he could find was light blue contact paper.

The race itself was headlined by an epic duel between Ford GT40, Cobra, Chaparral, Ferrari, and Porsche. Most memorable about the event was 5-plus inches of rain falling at the halfway point. The no. 37 TR4 finished 41st overall. (Photo Courtesy Cape Coventry Racing)

In his official capacity, Kastner's next task was to prep three TR4s for the 1964 Shell 4,000 Rally across Canada. His tuning and preparation skills were again validated when the Triumph TR4 team won the grueling five-day race from Vancouver to Montreal. From that success, Kastner went back to Sebring in 1965 to co-manage the factory Spitfire effort.

Kastner's main role as Competitions Manager was to ensure performance parts were readily available for anyone competing in their Triumph. He traveled the country extensively, waving the Triumph flag and sharing his tuning secrets.

KAS, PETE AND THE TR250K

The racing community is a tight-knit group and everyone knows everyone. Just before officially becoming Competitions Manager at Triumph, Kastner had accepted a position with Carroll Shelby and still had many friends there. One of them was Peter Brock.

Brock, best known for his designs for General Motors, including the Corvette Stingray (when he was just 19), was working for Shelby when he and Kastner first came up with the idea for a special Triumph racing car. Brock had designed the legendary Shelby Daytona Coupe and recently left Shelby to start Brock Racing Enterprises (BRE). They wanted to create a car that would make a dramatic impression on the racing world and help vault Triumph to be a racing powerhouse.

Kastner and Brock talked on and off about the Triumph racing special for several years. Prior to one of his many trips to headquarters, Kastner finally asked Brock to put pen to paper and create a rendering of the car they had been talking about. Legend has it that the design took less than an hour to create.

Kastner took the sketch of the low, aerodynamic, modern racing car to England and was able to sell Coventry brass on funding the effort using only the one drawing plus his racing resume and the promise of major media coverage. Before boarding his international flight, Kastner paid a visit to *Car and Driver* magazine. After sharing Brock's sketch and the promise of a scoop, Kastner was able to secure a feature article that included putting the TR250K on the cover. How could anyone say no?

Triumph was able to wring a small budget of just $25,000 out of the coffers and Kastner returned home to build a car for the 1968 12 Hours of Sebring.

The road-going TR250 was the U.S.-spec car of the day, so it was used as the base for the new racing car. "K" was added (for Kastner) and the project was dubbed TR250K. Kastner's role was to create the chassis and build the engine. Brock sourced materials to build the all-aluminum body.

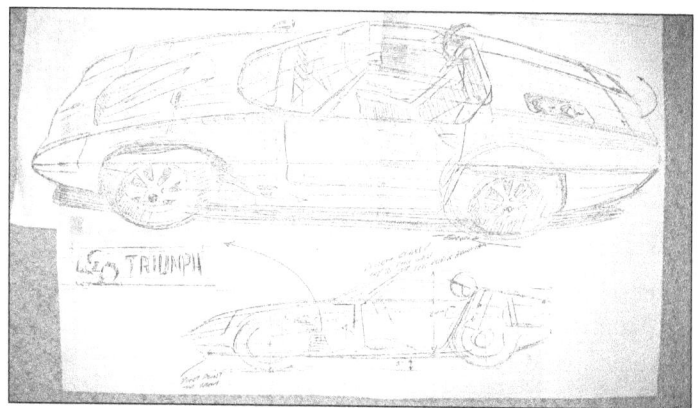

The sketch that launched a legend. Peter Brock's rendering of a radical new racing car designed specifically for the 12 Hours of Sebring endurance challenge. As legend has it, Brock drew this car in less than an hour after Kas Kastner told him he had an audience in Coventry, but time was tight. The design was the culmination of extensive talks between the two men musing about creating a Triumph that would make a statement on the track. (Photo Courtesy Kas Kastner)

The radical-looking TR250K. So named for the TR250 underpinnings with the "K" added for Kastner. The hand-formed aluminum bodywork was fitted to a stock TR250 frame sitting on stock suspension and powered by a stock drivetrain. The car qualified 39th and was categorized in the Sports Prototype group. Unfortunately, the car was retired early in the race when a rear wheel broke and irreparably damaged the suspension. Driver Jim Dittmore and the car were unhurt. (Photo Courtesy Peter Brock)

Kastner and his team performed their usual magic on the 2.5-liter 6-cylinder engine to boost performance. The factory Zenith-Stromberg carburetors were retained. To accommodate the low, swept-back bodywork and to improve balance, the engine was set well back into the chassis by 9 full inches. Brock's design was incredibly sleek and almost futuristic for its day. There was a lot of experimenting with aerodynamics during this time, and this design was the epitome of clean lines. It had a small movable spoiler at the rear to aid in downforce.

They worked frantically and the car was barely completed in time for the race. This meant that there was little time to put the car through its paces, so Sebring practice served as the only true testing. Bob Tullius and Jim Dittmore were the equivalent of test pilots when they stepped into the car for the first time. They spent most of the early part of the weekend chasing a variety of issues before qualifying in the lower third of the grid.

The TR250K was pitted against four factory Porsche 907s, with drivers including Vic Elford and Jo Siffert, as well as a Penske Camaro driven by Mark Donohue. Another

Instrumentation featured a Smiths tachometer sourced from the TR250, but Stewart-Warner gauges filled the center pod. The lever to the right of the stick shift allowed the driver to set the rear wing for more or less downforce. (Photo Courtesy Peter Brock)

The venerable Triumph 2.5-liter inline 6 fed by triple Weber 45DCOE carbs. Just like the Spitfire, the one-piece hood tipped forward to reveal the beautifully prepared 165-hp mill. To keep the low hood line, the engine was moved rearward in the frame by a full 9 inches. (Photo Courtesy Peter Brock)

CHAPTER 7: Triumph on Track

Pete Brock penned the shape of the TR250K. He is best known as the youngest designer at General Motors when he was hired at just 19 years old. Shortly thereafter he designed the Corvette Stingray. He departed to join the Shelby Cobra racing team and went on to design the Shelby Daytona Coupe. (Photo Courtesy Peter Brock)

The TR250K was a purpose-built racer using the latest technology in mid-1960s aerodynamics. It was a major departure from Brock's previous masterpiece: the curvaceous Cobra Dayton Coupe. The angular panels were designed to cut through the air and a moveable spoiler on the back allowed the driver to dial in downforce for any situation. (Photo Courtesy Peter Brock)

The car was built in 90 days and on a budget of $25,000. It debuted at the 1968 12 Hours of Sebring. The shape of things to come? Designed in 1968, it wasn't expressly designed as the next TR model, but some of the lines do resemble the TR7. (Photo Courtesy Peter Brock)

highly experimental car on the grid was the Howmet TX Turbine car.

Despite Tullius' and Dittmore's best efforts, the true potential of the car was never realized. The right rear hub broke just a few laps into the race. It was irreparable so the TR250K was retired.

Despite this disappointment Kastner was true to his promise of major media coverage. The TR250K appeared on the cover of the April 1968 issue of Car and Driver magazine.

The 12 Hours of Sebring turned out to be the car's only run. In the months following, the TR250K was featured at many shows around the country. Since then, it has traded hands several times and is now part of a private collection.

TULLIUS THE TENACIOUS

Bob Tullius was another privateer doing very well with his TR3 in the early 1960s. Based out of Fairfax, Virginia, he trailered his TR3 up and down the East Coast, where he raced and won many SCCA competitions.

Tullius, a Kodak salesman at the time, was a weekend warrior with a penchant for success. The secret to his success was impeccable preparation coupled with his strong driving skills. As Tullius continued his campaign on the track, he was also waging a campaign on Triumph's offices in New York. Tullius understood that racing was a rich man's sport and was looking for financial help. Specifically, he wanted a new TR4 to race in exchange for Triumph promotion on the track. He called Triumph's offices every single day.

Despite wanting to support Tullius, the ever-tight financial picture precluded Triumph from granting his request. Tullius' only play was to shame the prized new model. Tullius said that if he didn't receive a new TR4 he would go out and beat the new car in his old TR3. He did. Handily. He received a new TR4 in the following month.

It wasn't all magical from that point on. Tullius totaled the new TR4 in a racing accident shortly after receiving it. Of course, it was a stretch to get him a TR4 in the first place so a replacement would not be forthcoming from Triumph. Tullius and his team purchased several other crashed TR4s to assemble one competitive car from the parts. They promptly won every SCCA event they entered.

By this point, Tullius had given notice at Kodak to pursue a racing career. He was successful enough on the track that Triumph was sending him a small stipend for his racing efforts each weekend. It wasn't enough to operate the team, but Tullius could make a dollar go a long way. In an interview with Autoweek magazine he said, "If I received a dollar from a sponsor or manufacturer, I made sure they

Bob Tullius is the most celebrated Triumph racer and is synonymous with its racing success, even though he was not officially a partner to the factory.

The racing bug bit Tullius when he tried a racing school at the wheel of a TR3. He was immediately successful and was able to persuade Triumph of America to give him a new TR4 to campaign in SCCA events. Through his impeccable preparation, his speed on the track, and his salesmanship he was able to parlay it all into the Group 44 racing ream with the iconic white and green livery and Quaker State Motor Oil sponsorship. (Photo Courtesy Moss Motors)

During his 25-year run, Tullius campaigned a TR3, TR4, TR6, TR7, Spitfire, and GT6. One of the most recognized cars was the TR6, shown here in the corkscrew at Laguna Seca in a vintage racing event. Tullius took home the championship hardware in countless regional and national SCCA races. He was a savvy marketer as well and partnered with the dealers near the racetracks to bring greater media coverage. (Photo Courtesy John Lamm)

received a dollar and a half's worth of value back."

In 1964, Tullius won the first American Road Race of Champions at Riverside, California. The next year he moved his headquarters to Falls Church, Virginia, and officially launched Group 44 Racing. The name was born out of his racing number. Group 44 cars were turned out in white with drivers in crisp, white driving suits. There was no doubting the thoroughness of preparation.

In 1966, Tullius was able to secure Quaker State sponsorship for his team and the now-legendary dual green stripes were added to the livery of Group 44. He continued his practice of contacting local dealers prior to a race weekend to set up a promotion. Tullius appeared at the dealership with the race cars and the dealer could advertise the promotion, for which Tullius received a fee. Often, the name of the dealership appeared on the car during the race weekend.

During the next 10 years, Group 44 continued to receive and develop each new Triumph model, including the Spitfire, GT6, TR6, and eventually the TR7 and TR8. As the team grew so did the stable of cars, which included the Dodge

Tullius won the SCCA Championship and went on to race IMSA Camel GT and Trans-Am in a Jaguar XJR. Of course, his pursuit of performance was not confined to four wheels. Tullius became a pilot and avid enthusiast with his own P-51 Mustang. He is pictured here in the TR6 with Group 44 Chief Mechanic Brian Fuerstenau. (Photo Courtesy Moss Motors)

Dart, MGB, MG Midget, and Jaguar E-type.

Throughout the period, Tullius continued his winning ways. When the TR6 debuted in 1969, he won the very first race. And when the TR7 arrived in 1976, he won the first five races of the season.

CHAPTER 7: Triumph on Track

In 1977 and 1978, Tullius switched to a V-12 Jaguar E-Type and won back-to-back driver's championships. In 1979, Tullius returned to Triumph power in the new TR8, running a full International Motor Sports Association (IMSA) schedule. His final season with a Triumph was in 1980. Group 44 took the class win at Sebring, won five races during the season, and Tullius finished 2nd in points.

During its 25-year span, Group 44 Racing brought home 14 SCCA national titles, 3 Trans-Am championships, and 11 IMSA wins.

Through the years, many of the cars were sold and competed in other liveries; however, Tullius still has some of the cars and keeps them in his hangar at the Sebring airport.

CONRERO

Oh, what could have been.

In 1960, as the Competitions department was busily swapping out the new TRS body shell for the TR3S, the top brass at Standard-Triumph was looking to make a statement with a very special Le Mans racer. Unfortunately, internal people resources were not up to the challenge so the only choice was to commission a builder. Financial resources were also tight, but enough money was scraped together to commission Italian tuning expert Virgilio Conrero to build a car. In fact, four examples were commissioned with the goal of being more aerodynamic and looking more like the cars at the front end of the grid. Conrero is best known for his work with Alfa-Romeo throughout the 1960s.

Standard-Triumph shipped a TRS without the body to Conrero's facility in Turin, Italy. Conrero had a free hand to create whatever he wanted with the design. The only stipulation was the use of the Sabrina engine and to do it all within budget constraints. Unfortunately, the project was stillborn because money began to run out shortly after the project began. In the end, only one example of the car was completed.

The Conrero, as it is known, featured a tube frame on top of the TRS frame, which was wrapped in a lightweight alloy body. There is no denying that it is extremely reminiscent of Ferraris of the era. The styling was again designed by Michelotti, with the final product being built by Carrozzeria Vignale, also of Turin.

The car was supposed to be designed as a sports racer for the specific purpose of racing at Le Mans. However, the shape and attention to detail made it a very stylish sports coupe. The only real race-inspired element might be the oversize fuel filler located above the right rear wheel. True to the plan, the car was powered by the Sabrina engine, but Conrero ditched the SU carbs in favor of Weber twin-choke models. It's been said in many journals that this simple change made a significant difference in the performance of the Sabrina mill. The increase in performance and the

Oh, what could have been! Triumph commissioned Virgilio Conrero to create four special cars for the 1961 24 Hours of Le Mans. Conrero delivered a gorgeous aluminum body wrapped around a modern alloy tube frame. Powered by the 165-hp Sabrina engine, the shape of the car was as good as any GT car coming out of Italy at that time. Unfortunately, finances were tight and Leyland put the kibosh on the project with only one example built. (Photo Courtesy Moss Motors)

The car design was pure period-GT all the way around. The body sat low in the frame, resulting in a tall transmission tunnel. The tight layout resulted in the race-type fuel filler being ported through the rear glass. The interior was as luxuriously appointed as you would expect from a car styled in Italy, but the gauges and switchgear came from Triumph's parts bin, right down to the unique overdrive switch. (Photo Courtesy Moss Motors)

THE HUFFAKER TR7

Huffaker Engineering began as a racing chassis design and building company near Sears Point Raceway in Sonoma, California.

It was best known for its work on Jaguars, MGs, Austin Minis, Austin-Healeys, and Jensen Healeys. While its main business was customer cars, it also ran a number of cars under the Huffaker flag. Similar to those of Tullius, these cars were meticulously prepped for competition in SCCA D-, E-, and H-Production classes. Huffaker cars competed across the country and although they were available in many colors, the best-known and most successful cars were turned out in a gleaming tuxedo black.

In the late 1970s, Huffaker had been campaigning a TR7 coupe without a lot of success. In 1979, it was ready to try the TR8, but that was dropped due to a lack of TR8s in competition. The Huffaker team took a previously raced 1978 TR7 convertible and made it ready for competition.

Lee Mueller was chosen to drive the TR7. He had previously won national championships in an Austin-Healey Sprite and a Kastner-prepped Spitfire. Mueller chalked up a number of victories during the year and in the final race of the season he led flag-to-flag at Road Atlanta to capture the D-Production National Championship.

The Huffaker TR7 was built by Joe Huffaker and Joe Carr specifically for the SCCA national runoffs at Road Atlanta. The car was to be driven by Carr and Lee Mueller. Working four straight days and nights to finish the car, it was loaded into the trailer and without ever turning a wheel, Mueller put the TR7 roadster on the pole. He went on to win the D-Production championship. First race. Right out of the box. (Photo Courtesy Joe Huffaker)

decrease in weight make one wonder what could have been. And not only from a racing perspective but also what it might have done for Triumph road cars.

Conrero delivered the lone right-hand-drive car to Coventry in 1961, after the Competitions department had been closed down. The car was never raced and sat at the back of the factory for an undetermined amount of time. Eventually, the Conrero, along with any remaining TRSs, were sold to a private collector and the car has not been seen since.

Unfortunately, there are no records of the technical specifications of the car and only a handful of photos exist. The Sabrina engine is clearly visible under the hood and there is evidence of some Standard-Triumph switchgear in the interior.

The 2-liter twin-cam was still being promoted as the engine of the future. The Sabrina powerplant was shoehorned into the Conrero; it produced about 165 hp. Exhaust was piped down the left-hand side of the car and exited just ahead of the rear wheel. In true Italian styling aesthetics, the pipes ran inside the rocker panel with three vents to aid cooling. The twin-cam mill should have been enough to propel the GT car to 150 mph. (Photo Courtesy Moss Motors)

CHAPTER 7: Triumph on Track

POSTSCRIPT: THE TRIUMPH ACCLAIM

This piece begins just as many previous chapters began. Times were tough at British Leyland. It was the late 1970s and Leyland was scrambling to develop a number of new models across several different marques to ensure the corporation's survival into the new decade. Time was short, money was tight, and the pressure was too great to do it all in-house. Some of the work had to be outsourced.

British Leyland CEO Michael Edwardes was keenly aware of other car manufacturers collaborating, sometimes across international borders, to produce a multitude of cars under different badges but with the same base model. Even prior to Edwardes taking the reins, Leyland had already been in exploratory conversations with some of the other U.K.- and Europe-based carmakers. Unfortunately none of these talks bore fruit so Edwardes had to look more globally. Enter Honda Motor Company.

In 1978 British Leyland and Honda made a contract to produce a new economical family car for the British market. The goal was to build enough cars to bridge the gap until the new, homegrown line of family cars was ready to market under the Austin brand. The Austins would not be ready until 1983. In October 1981, the Triumph Acclaim was launched.

The car was based on the Honda Ballade (Civic in the United States), which was not yet being sold in Europe. It was positioned to replace the Triumph Dolomite sedan that ended production just as this deal was being signed. With the demise of the Dolomite, the Canley plant was shuttered.

The new Triumph was powered by the 1,335-cc transverse-mounted 4-cylinder from the patented Honda CVCC generation of engines. The 70 horses powered the front wheels through a 5-speed manual gearbox or an optional 3-speed automatic. To disguise the car's origins, the Honda-branded OHC cover was swapped out for a plain black cover.

All Honda markings were replaced with Triumph laurel badges. On the inside, seats were pulled from the Morris Ital, but the rest was all Honda.

The car was a hit. More than 133,000 units were sold between the autumn of 1981 and the summer of 1984. Production on the Acclaim stopped in favor of a new Rover 200, which was based on the next generation of Honda Ballades.

Yes, it was the last model to carry the Triumph name, but make no mistake, nothing about this car was linked to the Triumphs detailed on the preceding pages. No parts-bin sourcing, no carry-overs of chassis, or reused suspension that would make it a descendant of Triumph's greatest ancestors. In fact, you would be hard-pressed to find a Triumph enthusiast who acknowledges the Acclaim.

Because it did carry the Triumph badge, it could have claimed one last "first" in the history of the nameplate. The manufacture of the Acclaim marked the first time a Japanese car was assembled in Europe.

The 1981 Triumph Acclaim. It is just as it looks: a rebadged Honda Civic. In the late 1970s, British Leyland was looking for a new model to replace the TR7/TR8 but was woefully underfunded and lacking the ability to develop a new car. There was a lot of cross-badging happening in the industry and British Leyland began talks with Renault. When the Renault solution proved to be unworkable, it ended up in Japan.

Honda was just about to unveil a new Civic (Ballade in Britain) and a deal was struck to assemble the new cars in the Cowley plant as Triumphs. The cars actually have no link to the Triumph cars in this book except for a few badges and decals. More than 133,000 Acclaims were built between 1981 and 1984. (Photo Courtesy Simon Goldsworthy/*Triumph World*)

APPENDIX

PRODUCTION TOTALS

These numbers are for all U.S. and U.K. models.

Year	Model	Total
1946–1948	1800 Roadster	2,501
1948–1949	2000 Roadster	2,000
1953–1955	TR2	8,628
1955–1957	TR3	13,377
1957–1961	TR3A	57,936
1962	TR3B	3,331
1961–1965	TR4	40,253
1965–1967	TR4A	28,465
1967–1968	TR5	2,947
1967–1968	TR250	8,484
1968–1976	TR6	94,619
1975–1981	TR7	112,368

Year	Model	Total
1980–1981	TR8	2,722
1953–1955	Swallow-Doretti	273
1959–1961	Italia 2000GT	312
1962–1965	Spitfire Mark 1	45,753
1965–1967	Spitfire Mark 2	37,409
1967–1970	Spitfire Mark 3	65,320
1970–1974	Spitfire Mark IV	70,021
1974–1980	Spitfire 1500	95,829
1966–1968	GT6 Mark 1	15,818
1968–1970	GT6 Mark 2/GT6 Plus	12,066
1970–1973	GT6 Mark 3	13,042

RESOURCES AND RECOMMENDED READING

Triumph Cars: The Complete Story, by Graham Robson and Richard Langworth. Motor Racing Publications, England, 1979
Triumph Guide by Dave Allen and Dick Strome. Sports Car Press, 1959
The Triumph TRs: A Collector's Guide, by Graham Robson. Motor Racing Publications, England, 1978
Triumph Spitfire and GT6: A Collector's Guide, by Graham Robson. Motor Racing Publications, England, 1991
The Story of Triumph Sports Cars, by Graham Robson. Motor Racing Publications, England, 1973
Triumph by Name Triumph by Nature, by Bill Piggott. Dalton-Watson Publishing, England, 1996
Triumph Sport and Elegance, by Bill Piggott. Haynes Publishing, England, 2006
TR7: The Bullet that Backfired on British Leyland, by Steve Jackson. Lily Publications, England, 2015
Triumph Spitfire and GT6: The Complete Story, by Richard Dredge. The Crowood Press, England, 2014
Works Triumphs in Detail, by Graham Robson. Herridge & Sons, England, 2014
Triumph Cars in America, by Mike Cook. Motorbooks International, United States, 2001
Essential Triumph TR2–TR8, by David Hodges. Bayview Books, England, 1994
Triumph TR6, by William Kimberly, Veloce Publishing, England, 1995
TR for Triumph, by Chris Harvey, Haynes Publishing, England, 1983
Triumph Spitfire and GT6: A Collector's Guide, by Graham Robson, Motor Racing Publications, England, 1991
The Triumph TRs: A Collector's Guide, by Graham Robson, Motor Racing Publications, England, 1978
Triumph TR, by James Taylor, Motorbooks International, United States, 1997
MG by McComb, by F. Wilson McComb, Osprey Publishing, England, 1979
Healey: The Handsome Brute, by Chris Harvey, Haynes Publishing, England, 1982
Donald Healey: My World of Cars, by Peter Garnier, Patrick Stephens Limited, England, 1989
Standard Catalog of Imported Cars, by Mike Covello. Krause Publications, 2002
Sebring: The Official History of America's Great Sports Car Race by Ken Breslauer. David Bull Publishing, 1995

INDEX

A

Acclaim, 52, 124
Alpine Rally, 108
Alpine Trial, 16
American Road Race of Champions, 121
Andersen, Arthur, 34, 35
Andersen, Dorothy, 34
Autocar, 24, 57, 70, 96
Autosport, 88, 108

B

Ballard, Arthur, 21
Ballisat, Keith, 109, 114
Becquart, Marcel, 109
Belgrove, Walter, 15, 17, 24, 26, 27, 28, 29, 32, 44
Bettmann, Siegfried, 9, 10, 12, 13, 14, 16
Bicycles, 9, 10, 34
Black, John, 12, 18–23, 25–31, 34, 35, 40, 44, 45, 46, 57, 65, 66, 70, 71, 73, 76, 77, 78, 88, 89, 93, 97, 107, 108, 123, 124
BMC, 44, 47, 60, 63, 84, 89, 91, 108
Bolton, Peter, 109, 114, 117
Bonneville Salt Flats, 29, 106
British Leyland Motor Corporation, 63
British Motor Holdings, 63, 94
Brock Racing Enterprises, 118
Brock, Peter, 118, 119, 120
Brooke, Leslie, 106, 114
Brooklands, 18

C

Cal Sales, 34, 35, 117, 118
Cal Specialties, 34
Callaby, Frank, 21, 24
Car and Driver, 55, 57, 59, 78, 89, 118, 120
Car Life, 39
Carr, Joe, 123
Conrero, The, 122, 123
Conrero, Virgilio, 122, 123
Coventry Climax, 13, 14

D

Dawson Car Company, 10
Deen, Dorothy, 35, 117

Dick, Alick, 20, 30, 42, 44–47, 50, 55, 56, 84, 85, 108, 110, 125
Dickson, Bob, 106
Diehl, Ed, 117
Dittmore, Jim, 119, 120
Dolomite sedans, 76
Dolomite Straight Eight, 15, 16, 108
Dubois, Claude, 111

E

1800 Roadster, 21, 23, 24, 25
1800 Town and Country Saloon, 25
Earls Court Motor Show, 28, 29
Edwardes, Michael, 124

F

1500, 95, 96–98
Ferguson, Harry, 20, 25, 42, 55
Flying 8, 42, 43
Flying Nine, 28, 29
Flying 10, 43
Furstenau, Brian, 122

G

Gates, Charles, 35, 116, 117
Gatsonides, Maurice, 108, 114
Geneva car show, 29
Giesecke, Gerhart, 64, 66
Gloria Southern Cross, 13, 14, 16
Gloria Tourer, 14
Grant, Gregor, 108
Great Depression, 13, 14
Grinham, Ted, 25
Group 44 Racing, 121, 122
GT6, 69, 82, 97–105, 115, 121, 125
GT6 Mark 2, 98, 104
GT6 Mark 3, 82, 105
GT6 Plus, 98, 102, 104

H

Hadley, Bert, 106, 107, 108
Healey, Donald, 14–19, 28, 29, 34, 60, 87, 96, 106, 108, 125
Herald, 42, 44, 45, 46, 48, 57, 82, 84–88, 98
Hobbs, David, 110, 114, 116
Holbrook, Claude, 16, 18
Holland, Cyril, 11
Honda Motor Company, 124

Hopkirk, Paddy, 108, 116
Huffaker Engineering, 123
Huffaker TR7, 123

I

IMSA, 117, 121, 122, 123
Italia 2000GT, 48, 50, 95

J

Jabbeke Road, 29, 30, 107
Jaguar Rover Triumph Inc., 78

K

Kamm, Wunibald, 65
Karmann, Wilhelm, 64, 66
Kastner, R. W., 6, 35, 115–120
Kellner, Bruce, 117
Kimber, Cecil, 20

L

Le Mans, 33, 38, 46, 51, 91, 104, 106–117, 122
Lee, Tony, 6, 73, 123
Leyland Motors Ltd., 56
Liege-Rome-Liege rally, 108
Liverpool Motor Show, 69
Lloyd, John, 73
London Motor Show, 46, 84, 85
Los Angeles Examiner Grand Prix, 116
Lynx 2+2, 74
Lyons-Charbonnières rally, 108
Lyons, William, 11, 12, 19, 20, 22, 23, 26, 28, 46, 55

M

Macau Car, 116
Macau Grand Prix, 115
Mann, Harris, 75, 76
Markland, Stanley, 56, 85
Massey-Harris, 44
Maudslay, Reginald, 10, 12
Mayflower, 19, 25, 26, 28, 39, 40
Michelotti, Giovanni, 42, 44–53, 59, 63, 64, 73, 82, 84, 85, 86, 87, 94, 95, 98, 99, 101, 112, 114, 122
Mille Miglia, 33, 108, 114
Mitchell, Nancy, 108
Modern Motor, 88
Monte Carlo rally, 18, 107, 108
Morgan-Hastings, 13

Morris-Goodall, Mortimer, 106
Morris, William, 10, 11, 124
Motor, 32, 62
Motor Sport, 18
Motor Trend, 78
Mueller, Lee, 123
Mulliners coachbuilders, 24, 25, 55

N

Newnham, Maurice, 18

P

Paris auto show, 26
Prestwich, J. A., 10
Project Bomb, 84–105
Project Bullet, 26, 27, 72, 73, 74, 76, 79, 80, 81
Project Zest, 44, 45, 46, 48, 50, 51, 52, 113
Project Zobo, 44, 45, 84, 85
Project Zoom, 44, 45, 46, 47, 48, 50, 51, 113

R

RAC Rally, 33, 108
Redwood Empire amateur race, 113
Renown Saloon, 25, 26
Richardson, Ken, 28, 29, 30, 35, 106–110, 112, 114, 116
Riverside, 121
Road & Track, 33, 37, 55, 62, 63, 70, 76, 78, 79, 80, 95, 105
Road Atlanta, 123
Robson, Graham, 112, 113, 125
Rothschild, Mike, 117
Royal Automobile Club, 10, 11, 33, 108
Ruffino S.p.A., 50

S

Sabrina, 45–49, 51, 110, 111, 112, 114, 122, 123
Sanderson, Ninian, 106, 109, 111
Sears Point Raceway, 123
Sebring, 106, 116–120, 122, 125
Shell 4,000 Rally, 118
Slotemaker, Rob, 108, 110, 114, 116
Snell Foundation, 113
Snell, Howard, 113
Snively, Howard, 113

Soisbault, Annie, 108
Southern Cross, 13, 14, 16, 18
Southern Cross Monte Carlo, 16
Spitfire 1500, 95, 98
Spitfire 4, 84, 86, 87, 88, 91, 98, 99
Spitfire Mark 1, 84
Spitfire Mark 2, 89, 98
Spitfire Mark 3, 7, 104
Spitfire Mark IV, 103, 105
Sports Car Club of America, 97, 106, 107, 113, 116, 117, 120–123
Stag, 69, 79, 82, 83, 95, 103
Standard Motor Company, 10, 12
Standard Nine, 11
Standard-Swallow, 11, 12
Story of Triumph Sports Cars, 125
Sulke, Walter, 115
Super Eight, 14
Super Nine, 13, 14
Super Seven, 13, 14
Swallow Doretti, 34, 117
Swallow Sidecar and Coachbuilding Company, 11
Sykes, Norma, 110

T

12 Hours of Sebring, 116, 117, 118, 120
2000 Roadster, 25
2000 sedan, 57, 59, 60, 62, 82, 83, 84, 20TS, 28–31
24 Hours of Le Mans, 51, 106, 110, 114, 116, 122
10/20, 10, 11
15, 11
13/30, 11
1300, 82
Tokyo Motor Show, 95
Tourist Trophy, 33
TR1, 28, 29
TR2, 29–34, 36, 37, 39, 41, 59–63, 70, 75, 102, 104, 106–109, 114, 117–120, 125
TR3, 35–42, 44–49, 52, 53, 54, 56, 58, 84, 86, 108, 110, 111, 113, 117, 120, 121
TR3 Dream Car, 45
TR3A, 37, 39, 40, 41, 45, 46, 47, 49, 50, 51, 85, 108, 110, 111, 112, 116
TR3B, 35, 40, 47, 85

TR3S, 32, 33, 39, 71, 108–110, 112, 117, 122
TR4, 35, 39, 41, 44, 46, 47, 48, 50–60, 63, 65, 85, 87, 88, 89, 91, 112, 113, 114, 117, 118, 120, 121
TR4A, 56, 57, 59, 60, 61, 69, 104
TR5, 59–63, 66, 102, 104
TR6, 64–74, 121, 125
TR7, 71–74, 76–82, 98, 120, 121, 123, 124, 125
TR8, 79, 80, 81, 121–125
TR250, 59–63, 70, 102, 104, 118, 119
TR250K, 118, 119, 120
TR-X, 26, 27, 28
Trans-Am, 121, 122, 128
Triumph Motor Company, 18
Triumph motorcycles, 9, 10, 11, 16, 18
Triumph Over Triumph, 28
Triumph World, 13, 17, 24, 25, 43, 45, 72, 73, 124
TRS, 35, 42, 50, 51, 53, 72, 79, 85, 93, 107, 108, 109, 111–114, 117, 122, 125
Tube Investments Company, 34
Tulip Rally, 108
Tullius, Bob, 69, 114, 116, 117, 119–123
Turin Motor Show, 49

V

Van Damm, Sheila, 29
Vanguard, 20, 25–29, 33, 35, 36, 38, 39, 40, 53, 60, 64
Victoria, 10
Vignale Carrozzeria, 44, 47

W

Waddington, John, 108
Wadsworth, Edgar, 109
Wallwork, Johnny, 108
Walmsley, William, 11
Ward, Thomas, 18, 19
Webster, Harry, 44, 52, 64, 82, 99, 110, 112, 113, 116
Weymann bodies, 18, 19, 21, 23, 42, 46, 52, 87

Additional books that may interest you...

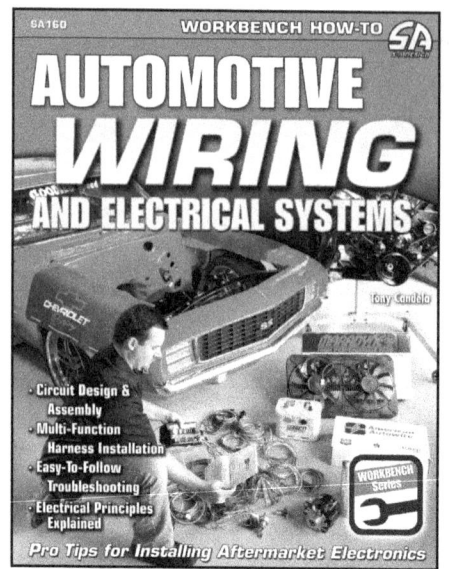

MOTORAMA: GM's Legendary Show & Concept Cars *by David Temple* Motorama expert and experienced author David Temple has comprehensively researched the show, the cars, and the personalities to create a fascinating story with new photos of these magnificent cars. Temple goes into detail on the body, frame, engine, drivetrain, and special features of each showcase model. He has also retraced the ownership histories of some of these cars. This book features fascinating period photography of Motorama cars at the show, in development, and at different locales. No other automotive show rivaled the extravagant and elaborate Motorama for stunning productions and awe-inspiring cars. Hardbound, 8.5 x 11 inches, 192 pages, 400 color and b/w photos. ***Item # CT533***

AUTOMOTIVE WIRING AND ELECTRICAL SYSTEMS *by Tony Candela* This is the perfect book to unshroud the mysteries of automotive electrics and electronic systems. The basics of electrical principles, including voltage, amperage, resistance, and Ohm's law, are revealed in clear and concise detail, so you can understand what these mean in the construction and repair of automotive electrical circuits. All the tools and the proper equipment required for automotive electrical tasks are covered. In addition, this in-depth guide explains how to perform more complex tasks, such as adding new circuits, installing aftermarket electronics, repairing existing circuits, building your own wiring harness, and troubleshooting. Softbound, 8.5 x 11 inches, 144 pages, 350 color photos. ***Item # SA160***

DAVID KIMBLE'S CUTAWAYS *by David Kimble* This book reveals the secrets, techniques, procedures, and the dedication to craft that is required to produce these amazing illustrations. Kimble covers the step-by-step procedures while producing fresh artwork for this book featuring a McLaren Can-Am car as well as a vintage Harley-Davidson. Although the procedures covered here are unique to Kimble, and pretty much a pipe dream to mere mortals, this title provides an inside look into how he does it. Also included are the stories and tales of how it all started, traveling the world to illustrate cars, behind the scenes with manufacturers, the Corvette years, as well as a gallery of many illustrations. Never before has David Kimble shared the procedures for bringing these beautiful technical illustrations to life. Hardbound, 11 x 8.5 inches, 192 pages, 210 color images. ***Item # CT535***

Check out our website:

CarTechBooks.com

✓ **Find our newest books before anyone else**

✓ **Get weekly tech tips from our experts**

✓ **Featuring a new deal each week!**

LOST ROAD COURSES *by Martin Rudow* Many road courses were built in the 1950s and 1960s, the golden age of American road racing. These classic road courses built and hosted famous races, but did not survive the times. In the pages of this book, a nostalgic tour of these famous races at these vintage road circuits unfolds. Many period photos illustrate the racing action and the tracks themselves in their former glory, and modern color shows the tracks as they currently stand. If you're a fan of classic sports car, Can-Am, Trans-Am, IndyCar, Formula 1, as well as classic and unique tracks of yesteryear, this book is a must-have. Softbound, 8.5 x 11 inches, 144 pages, 350 color and b/w photos. ***Item # CT549***

Exclusive Promotions and Giveaways at www.CarTechBooks.com!

www.cartechbooks.com or 1-800-551-4754

www.ingramcontent.com/pod-product-compliance
Lightning Source LLC
Chambersburg PA
CBHW081458070526
44586CB00019B/2419